EMAIL MARKETING THAT DOESN'T SUCK

EMAIL MARKETING

THAT DOESN'T SUCK

HAVE FUN WRITING EMAILS YOUR SUBSCRIBERS WILL WANT TO READ (AND THAT WILL ACTUALLY MAKE YOU MONEY!)

BOBBY KLINCK

LIONCREST
PUBLISHING

Hardcover ISBN: 978-1-5445-2739-0
Paperback ISBN: 978-1-5445-2737-6
eBook ISBN: 978-1-5445-2738-3

For my wife, Kristy, and daughter, Kinsley,
who are my forever whys.

CONTENTS

INTRODUCTION

SINCE YOU'RE READING THIS BOOK, I'm guessing that you suck at email.

This just in: my editor says I should *not* accuse my readers of sucking at email. Fine, how about this…because you're reading this book, I'm guessing you want to get better at email.[1] Well, kudos to you for recognizing that your emails aren't great and for looking to figure out how to make them suck a little less.

And I've got good news for you: I used to *really* suck at email too. I'm talking "no one should have been subjected to the drivel I sent out" levels of suck.

Like pretty much every online marketer, I'd heard about the power of email marketing and that the strength of my business was directly tied to the size of my email list. I knew that I was always supposed to be list building. That I was supposed to be sending an email each and every week. Although I wasn't entirely clear on *how* I was supposed to be doing this, like a good student, I tried to follow the rules. I tried to do what the gurus told me.

Each and every week, I would send an email to my list telling them about my new podcast episode. These emails summed up the topic of that week's episode and provided some bullet-point highlights from the show that were designed to create curiosity.

---

1. That is, unless you happen to be my mom, who obviously bought this book to support her son. If that's you…Hi, Mom! (And sorry for the foul language that is to follow.)

But no matter what framework I followed or how consistent I was, email marketing didn't seem to be working (and it sure as hell wasn't making me any money!). Things were so bad that I was starting to question whether or not email was really dead. Luckily, I had a couple of friends help me get my head out of my ass and realize that email marketing wasn't the problem…I was!

The trouble was that I was writing emails that were boring with a capital B. They had no personality, no stories, no hint of who I actually am, none of the rhetorical flair that you've already experienced in this book. My emails could have come from *anyone*.

To prove this point, I could let you see pretty much *any* email I wrote in the early days. So I threw a dart at a list, and here's the example you get to see of the sucky way I *used* to write emails:

From: Bobby Klinck

Date: July 17, 2018

Subject: [Podcast Episode Alert] How To Name Your Business

Hey Jillian,[2]

Happy Tuesday from McAllen, Texas (heading back to DC later today).

(continued on page xi)

---

2. The email actually had a wildcard, so it was specifically addressed to each subscriber. Because my friend Jillian is the person who told me to tell stories rather than send boring emails, I'll be using her name as the subscriber for all emails in this book.

(continued from page x)

Often one of the first (and most critical) decisions you'll make as an entrepreneur is choosing a name for your business... or your podcast... or your blog... or your product...

If you're like most entrepreneurs, you did A LOT of thinking, brainstorming, and maybe even some spitballing to choose the name.

But way TOO many online entrepreneurs miss the next step... making sure they can legally use the name.

Business names, slogans, and logos (pretty much all branding) is protected by an area of law known as trademark law. And, as a general rule, the first person or company to use the name has the exclusive right to use the name for that area of business.

This is an issue that trips so many entrepreneurs up, so I figured it would be a good topic for a podcast mini-training.

This week's episode of The Online Genius Podcast[3] is all about the legal steps you need to take when you are naming your business.

When you give it a listen, you'll discover:

- What you need to do in the beginning to avoid trademark problems down the road.

- Three places to run a trademark search for the name you want to use.

- How to protect your name once you've chosen it.

(continued on page xii)

---

3. As of the time of this writing, I'm still creating my podcast each and every week, but we've renamed it *The Certified BADA$$ Online Marketing Podcast*. If you enjoy the wisdom, approach, and snark in this book and are a podcast listener, I'm gonna say you'll really enjoy the podcast. So, you know, go give it a listen. You can find it at www.bobbyklinck.com/podcast.

(continued from page xi)

- Why you definitely want to hire a lawyer (but not me!) to help you file a trademark application.

- Common areas of concern where trademark law can come up.

- And more.

You'll walk away from the episode knowing what you need to do to make sure you can legally use the name you've chosen for your business. Pretty cool, huh?

Click Here To Listen To The Show

Talk later.

Bobby

P.S. If you are enjoying the podcast, I would love for you to share it with your friends. All you have to do is forward this email to anyone that you know that you think should give the podcast a listen.

Bobby's Swift Kick in the Ass

You will see boxes like this throughout the book, with extra little tidbits of information and wake-up calls.

Here, I want to point out that any typos or errors you see in the example emails I've included within each chapter are intentional…Well, they weren't exactly *intentional* when I sent the emails, but that's exactly how those emails went out to subscribers. And I want to show you the emails exactly as they went out, not sanitized and proofed by the professional editors working on this book. (You'll see why in an upcoming chapter!)

Hey, wake up! It's over!

Like I said, these emails were *painfully boring*. I mean, I practically fell asleep just reformatting that email for this book. My editor was worried that including such a boring-ass email this early on might make readers run away screaming, thinking I don't know how to write emails. That's a fair concern, but I overruled said editor because you deserve to know how truly *awful* my emails used to be. My emails used to be where fun went to die; they were the best subscriber repellant that money could buy.

And, unlike my editor, I know that seeing how shitty my emails *used* to be will actually make you more likely to keep reading! I mean, you've got to be wondering how someone who was that ridiculously bad at email could flip the switch to the point that copywriters have "Bobby" folders where they save all my emails for inspiration.

Just as importantly, you needed to read that email to understand that writing emails people *want* to read didn't come naturally to me. The way I see it, you should take comfort in how bad I sucked because it proves there's hope for everyone… even you!

GOD DELIVERED A KICK IN THE ASS…IN THE FORM OF A PHOTOBOMB

There's another reason I shared that email with you: to show that you can change things seemingly overnight. If you noticed, I sent that email in July 2018. Just a few weeks later, on August 28, 2018, I sent what is among my most famous emails. Yup,

I went from mind-numbingly boring Bobby to email famous that quickly.

That August, I had the chance to hang out with Amy Porterfield (and four hundred or so other badass online friends) at her Entrepreneur Experience. The event was like a homecoming for me because it was filled with people I'd been hanging out with online for the past six months, but, up to that point, I'd never met any of them in person. One of the "new" friends I met at the event was a content strategist from Australia named Jillian Bowen. We clicked immediately, at least in part because we are both *a wee bit snarky*. Jillian also happens to have a quality I seek out in my friends: she isn't afraid to take me down a notch (or seven).

The night before the event started, there was a welcome reception with Amy and her team. The line to get a picture with Amy (she's kind of a big deal!) seemed to go on for miles. When I got to the front of the line, I finally met Chloe, one of Amy's key team members, in person, and I insisted that we take a picture together. She took a selfie using my phone because I'm useless when it comes to selfies. The rest of the night was a blur of meeting new friends, grabbing dinner, having drinks, and generally enjoying being together with hundreds of like-minded people.

When I got back to my room, I started looking through the pictures on my phone, and I had a deep belly laugh when I saw the selfie I'd taken with Chloe:

There was Amy, photobombing us with her tongue out! The picture was so hilarious that I *had* to share it with someone, but all of my new friends had retired for the evening. What's a guy supposed to do?

I did the only logical thing: I texted it to my wife.

Because the event was on the West Coast and we live on the East Coast, my wife was long asleep by the time I sent her the text. The next morning, I woke up to her simple—but pointed—response: "Why are you sending me pictures of you with random women?!?"

Whoops! She knew about Amy, but it never occurred to me that she didn't know what Amy looked like. So my wife literally thought I was just sending her pictures of me having a great time with random women. Yikes! Luckily, I was able to use my lawyering skills to convince my wife *not* to change the locks while I was away.

The next day, after hearing a speaker at the event talk about how we should include stories in our emails, I told my new friend Jillian how I had almost ruined my marriage by sending the photobomb to my wife. Jillian looked me straight in the eye and said something like "I think we know what your next email needs to be."

Although I often make unwise decisions, I am smart enough to take wise counsel. So I followed Jillian's advice and sent this email to my list the following week:

From: Bobby Klinck

Date: August 28, 2018

Subject: Why are you sending me pictures of you with random women?!

Hey Jillian,

I don't know about you, but I would love to find ways to help me make my business work more like clockwork (so maybe I could take some time away from the computer…). That's what this week's podcast episode is all about.

(continued on page xvii)

(continued from page xvi)

But first, I want to tell you about something funny that happened this weekend…

On Saturday, I woke up and checked my phone to find a text from my wife that said:

"Why are you sending me pictures of you with random women?!?"

Before you get worried for my safety, I wasn't in Vegas…

And, no, I hadn't done something monumentally stupid and accidentally sent photographic evidence to my wife.

That would be a crazy story… but that's not what happened.

Nope. I had sent what I thought was a funny photo of me from the Entrepreneur Experience that Amy Porterfield was hosting for about 400 like-minded Entrepreneurs in San Diego.

Since you are on my list, I'm guessing you probably know who Amy is. I mean she was on my podcast… I was on her podcast… And, you know, she's a kind of a big deal.

But I digress…

Here's the picture at issue:

(continued on page xviii)

(continued from page xvii)

Yeah, that's right... that's Amy Porterfield photobombing me!

But this isn't an email about Amy...

While I'm guessing that most of you know who Amy is, you may not know who I am actually posing with in this photo.

She's who this email is really about... and you really should know who she is.

That's Chloe. She's Amy's "Integrator."

If you aren't familiar with the term "Integrator," maybe you've heard of a project manager.

Well, Chloe is that a[4] so much more. She makes sure that things get done!

I don't know about you, but I could REALLY use someone like that in my business. One of my commitments from the event is that I am going to be building my team (if you know anyone...).

We can't do it all ourselves... especially not if we want to have a business that runs like clockwork.

That brings me back to this week's podcast episode...

In this week's episode of The Online Genius Podcast, I talk with Mike Michalowicz about turning your business into a well-oiled machine.

Mike is the best-selling author behind The Pumpkin Plan, The Toilet Paper Entrepreneur, Surge, and Profit First.

(continued on page xix)

---

4. There's one of those typos I mentioned. My team insisted that I put this footnote here to show you that, yes, we are aware of the typo, and *no* it is not my team's fault. Moving on...

(continued from page xviii)

Last week, he released his latest book, Clockwork: Design Your Business to Run Itself.

I don't know about you, but I would LOVE to get my business to run itself. That's why I was so excited to get a chance to interview Mike about the book.

Mike shared some incredible value, including this counterintuitive thought: "If we simply focus on doing more and being more productive, we'll keep packing and packing more and more work until we become impacted with work and then we're in real trouble."

He also laid out the seven-step method he's developed for making your business work like clockwork so you can start to build a business that doesn't require you to be there all the time!

Click here to check out this week's interview with Mike Michalowicz.

Talk later.

Bobby

P.S. As an epilogue to the story about the picture and my wife's response, you don't have to worry about my marriage. My wife knows who Amy is (but not by sight) and laughed (not sure if it was at me or with me) when I explained the story to her. But I think I've developed a new rule for life... Don't send your wife pictures of you with other women without explaining who they are!

P.P.S. The Entrepreneur Experience was kind of a world changing experience for me, so be on the lookout for some changes in the coming weeks and months.

After sending that email, a really weird thing happened: people responded! And not just one or two—countless long-time followers responded, telling me that they had laughed out loud and that my email made their day. Then, of course, there were the guys on my list who *apparently* thought I was responding to an email they had sent. Yep, multiple guys on my list thought they had been hacked and were sending *me* pictures of random women. Whoops again!

At any rate, the response told me that maybe I was onto something with this new style of email. *I was writing emails my audience actually wanted to read.*

ENOUGH WITH THE SHENANIGANS...WHAT ABOUT MAKING *MONEY*???

Yeah, yeah, yeah. I get that you might be here because of the whole "make some money" thing that my team insisted we put into the subtitle of the book.

Because you're reading this book (or perusing the Intro to decide whether or not you want to buy it), it's probably safe to assume that you want to make money with your email. The good news is that when you start writing emails people actually want to read, those emails tend to make you some money too.

Shocking, I know. But when you do email right, you can make money appear out of nowhere with quick, email-only promotions. And I'm not just talking about selling low-dollar offers. With the right approach to email, I was able to sell my signature $997 offer by sending a few emails. In 2019 alone, my email promotions of that one product generated about $200,000 in revenue. Not bad for a *single* product sold by a *one-man* operation.

About now, the jaded online marketer in you is probably

thinking something like "Sure, but you were probably marketing to a huge email list *and* you probably had an offer that's way cooler than mine!" While I get the skepticism, I assure you that nothing could be further from the truth. Throughout 2019, I was emailing a list that hovered around 5,000 people, and I was selling the most boring thing ever—legal templates.[5] The magic in my email promotions wasn't that I had a huge list or a really exciting offer; the magic came from the fact that I was doing email right and doing it right consistently.

Email marketing can make you good money—you just have to do it right. And that's what this book is about: showing you how to do email right.

Maybe you know that you need to be using email marketing in your business, but you're not doing it yet. Or you're emailing your list, but it's more about checking off a box instead of being intentional with how you use email. Maybe every time you sit down to write an email, you are faced with that damn cursor blinking in your face, taunting you from the top of a blank page. Or you're trying to send emails, and you're trying to do it right, but you're thinking, "It's so hard, and I don't know what to write, and nobody even reads my emails anyway, so this just sucks."

If people aren't opening your emails, why don't you try writing better emails—emails that people actually *want* to read? (Sounds

---

5. My accountant friends sometimes try to argue that their products are even more boring… but they're wrong. Is accounting boring? Uh, yeah! But at least their products are directly related to money. That makes them way less boring than legal policies and agreements that *no one* will ever read.

simple, right? But if it were that simple, everybody would be doing it.) Your emails don't *have* to suck. *Writing* emails doesn't have to suck either, and it doesn't have to be hard. I'll show you how in later chapters.

And when it becomes easier to write emails that are interesting, and that people want to read, and that get you responses—then your subscribers will be more likely to buy what you have to offer. In other words, that's what will allow you to make more money *and* better serve the people you built your business around helping in the first place.

Bobby's Swift Kick in the Ass

On my group coaching call this week, someone brought up a Big Name Marketer who talks about tips and tricks to increase open rates and engagement—things like splitting up emails to send in bursts and the ideal day or time to send emails. She asked me what I thought.

I replied, "You could do all of that...or you could just write better emails."

Let me be very clear, right up front: you may be expecting me to talk about those fancy tricks, but I'm not going to. All of those BS tactics make people think that there is some way to game the system, but the only trick that really works is *writing emails that don't suck.*

When you write good emails, none of that other crap matters.

WHO THIS BOOK IS FOR

I'm big on leveling with my people, so I want to make absolutely crystal clear who should buy this book…and who should put it back on the shelf.[6]

My brand and the businesses I serve are what I call "knowledge brands." We are businesses that sell our expertise. Our offers differ, but the common theme is that people buy our products or services based largely on their decision to trust us to guide them on their journey.

When customers are deciding whether to hire you for your expertise (or comparing you to "competitors"), they generally aren't going down a list of features and specifications. The buying decision is considerably more emotional. People will buy from you because they see you as an authority and because they have built a connection with you.

If you're building a knowledge brand, your marketing plan needs to involve building that authority and connecting with your audience. And email marketing is (in my humble opinion) the single best way to build a connection with your audience. This book will show you how to build connection using email… and how to then use it to sell with email.

If you are a coach, course creator, consultant, strategist, service provider, professional, or any other kind of brand that thrives on personal connections, this book is for you.

---

6. If you're someone who read that sentence and naturally expects me to follow up by spouting a bunch of platitudes that come down to how this is a book for anyone who wants to be successful and isn't for people who are lazy…*then this book is most definitely for you!* The *only* people who are that jaded are people well versed in the information product industrial complex (a.k.a. the people hell-bent on convincing you that you can get rich with an online information business).

THIS BOOK ISN'T FOR THE TIMID

Did you see the warning label on the back of the book? The one that told you that you shouldn't buy this book if you're an online marketing guru, member of the grammar police, or someone who can't handle a curse word or two? I am 100 percent serious about that warning because this book is written unapologetically in my true voice.

Luckily, I've got some crib notes to help me explain exactly what that means. Specifically, I have a "Voice Guide" that was prepared by a copywriter named Justin Blackman to help other people on my team capture my voice.[7] He dove into things I've written (largely my emails) and analyzed them six ways from Sunday to define my voice. Justin has this process down to a science (literally, he has charts and graphs). I'm guessing he anticipated working with me would be a typical project. Little did he know, nothing about me is typical. As my team and my editor can attest…I have a tendency to break *everything*.

And, apparently, my voice breaks the mold. The report Justin created leads off the section describing my voice with this: "Much like everything else he does, Bobby's voice doesn't fit into a 'traditional mold.' Instead, he takes the best pieces of various voices and comes up with something new."

Normally, Justin classifies people's voice type into a number of established categories, but not me. He had to *make up an entirely new category to describe how I write*.

Justin's conclusion is that I'm like your "big brother at the bar." He continued with this little gem: "Bobby is the adult

---

7. If you have others who write for you, I cannot recommend Justin highly enough. His company is called Pretty Fly Copywriting, and his work is pretty damn fly in my book.

version of the kid in the back of the class who made his friends laugh—but also asked smart questions back to the teacher."

When you dig into what that means, there are three really defining characteristics of my voice:

1. I will always fight *against* the status quo (because I tend to think most of the surface-level advice is garbage).

2. I'm fiercely protective of my people, which means I nurture and share every lesson I can (almost like a parent, but more relatable and less grown-up…you know, like a big brother).

3. I'm a snarky goofball.

Here's what that means in the context of this book.

The first two elements mean there are no sacred cows that I won't slay. This book challenges much of the status quo advice you've heard, not just about email marketing but about marketing more generally. I'm not doing that to attack the people who're teaching the status quo. I'm doing it because I'm like that protective big brother who doesn't want to see his kid brothers and sisters get hurt. And I'm willing to rock the boat, make waves, and burn bridges with the establishment if that's what it takes for me to protect you, my reader. Or, put another way, if you're one of those online marketing gurus who is spreading those false beliefs (or happen to love one of those folks), this book might be a bit uncomfortable for you.

The snarky goofball means that this book does not take itself too seriously. As a natural-born troublemaker (a.k.a. the kid in the back of the class), I learned long ago that a bit of humor goes a long way. Even if it's bad humor. And especially if it's at my own expense. I'm most certainly not a comedian, but like any good nerdy troublemaker, I learned long ago that making fun of myself defuses attacks that would otherwise be coming my way. You'll notice a lot of footnotes in this book, but very few of them are substantive. Think of them as your daily dose of nonsense that might just give you a chuckle.

Finally, the whole snarky goofball thing also means this book is most definitely not written in perfect English. Here's guessing you've already noticed that. You'll be barraged with split infinitives, dangling participles, colloquialisms, shifting parts of speech, sentence fragments, run-on sentences, and who the hell knows what other grammatical errors.[8] That's my long way of saying that if grammatical errors make your head hurt, I'm gonna suggest that you go ahead and put this book down. (See, there's at least a colloquialism and preposition to end that single sentence! Things do not get better from here…)

If you're someone who's open to new ideas about email marketing and are up for some fun, then keep reading!

HOW THIS BOOK IS STRUCTURED

So how do you get from "I suck at email" to "I love email"? Read on.

---

8. I would say my editor knows, but I'm pretty sure she threw up her hands before she even got to this footnote. Like I said, footnotes are the non-sense!

I've divided the book into two parts. In Part I, we'll dive into some key shifts you need to make in how you approach email marketing for it to work. In Part II, we'll cover how to approach your subscribers from the moment they join your list until the time you sell to them. Throughout, you'll discover:

- How to write emails in a way that makes sense for you.

- How to tell stories instead of being an email-generating robot.

- How to make your emails more interesting and relatable.

- That it's not the size of your list (or even how exciting your offer is) that matters; what matters is sending the right emails to the right people in the right order—and how to do it.

Before you decide to skip ahead to the chapter on selling so you can see how to make more money, just know that it doesn't work that way. The key to selling with email is in what happens *before* you ever start selling. This book is written in a deliberate order, so don't skip ahead to the good stuff—as you'll see, it's all good stuff,[9] *and* I've included plenty of stories and examples of my emails that you won't want to miss!

I do want you to understand that this book isn't meant to be a complete how-to guide to email marketing. Because, you know, there's only so much we can cover in a single book. About now, the jaded marketer in you is probably expecting me to

---

9. Why, yes, Humble *is* my middle name. Why do you ask?

come for your wallet. Most authors are like drug dealers these days: the book is meant to get you hooked so they can sell you something way more expensive where they share the actually *useful* information.

I am not your typical online entrepreneur (or typical author). We have a page where you can download all of my email resources, absolutely free. Yes, free. No catch. No trick. No upsell. (When you read Chapter 1, you'll understand more about why…)

Head over to www.bobbyklinck.com/email to download all my best email swipe and to grab your spot in my online course, BADA$$ Email Marketing. Think of this book as your overview and the resources on that page as your totally *free* how-to guide.

PART I

EMAIL MARKETING FUNDAMENTALS

BEFORE WE DIVE INTO WHAT YOU DO OR DO NOT KNOW about email and email marketing, my editor has suggested that I should tell you a thing or two to bolster my credibility. I wanted to just say, "I graduated with honors from Harvard Law School." But my party-pooper editor informs me that my fancy law degree is cool and all, but it has nothing to do with email marketing. Apparently, you might just be completely confused about how someone could go from Harvard lawyer to email badass. Fair point, so allow me to explain.[10]

---

10. Luckily, unlike Inigo Montoya, I have the time to explain instead of having to just sum up!

MY JOURNEY FROM LAWYER TO MARKETER

I graduated from Harvard Law School in 2002, and the first twelve years of my career were experiences that looked great on a résumé, including:

- A prestigious clerkship with the Honorable Richard S. Arnold on the United States Court of Appeals. Judge Arnold was one of the greatest liberal judges never to serve on the Supreme Court.[11]

- Working for a prominent law firm in Washington, DC, where one of my mentors was a lawyer I just called Neil at the time, but who I now have to refer to as Supreme Court Justice Neil Gorsuch.

- An illustrious gig as a federal prosecutor, where I got to stand up every day and say, "Robert Klinck on behalf of the United States of America."[12]

- Working at a small plaintiff's firm where I went up against the biggest defense firms in the country and kicked their asses up and down the court.

---

11. Judge Arnold was among the finalists President Clinton considered appointing both times there was a vacancy on the Supreme Court when he was president. So, no, I'm not just making up a story about him being a well-thought-of judge.

12. Yes, my formal name is Robert, but the only person who calls me that is my mom when she's mad at me...which will probably happen as soon as she sees the curse words in this book!

Even though I seemed very much like your typical, boring lawyer—putting on a suit and tie to get paid to argue with people all day—that's never who I was as a person. Quite the contrary.

Growing up, I was the consummate rebel. I was the kid who wore purple Doc Martens (before they were cool) and flannel shirts in a town where Wranglers and Justin Roper boots were the norm. I was in a punk rock band starting my sophomore year in high school, and I accepted the trophy for winning the state debate tournament wearing a Charlie Brown T-shirt and blue jeans. So you can probably imagine that I chafed showing up as a boring lawyer.

Even suiting up as a lawyer, I still felt very much like that rebellious kid.

My Unexpected Turn to Entrepreneurship

In 2014, I left my job to strike out on my own with Klinck LLC. It wasn't something I had planned, but I leapt in with both feet. Exactly one client came with me (yes, it was pretty much my very own *Jerry Maguire* moment), and that case settled relatively quickly.

And then I found myself with a lot of time and not a lot of work.

You'd be forgiven for thinking that a guy with a Harvard Law degree and my fancy-schmancy credentials would have no trouble building a law firm. But you'd be wrong. All my technical skills as a lawyer weren't worth squat because I didn't have the first clue how to market myself.

Ever the student, I started reading marketing books for lawyers. How do I put this gently? The nicest thing I can say is that lawyers are shitty marketers. They think marketing means writing articles for other lawyers, schmoozing other lawyers, and sending out the world's most boring newsletters to *other lawyers*. They missed the whole "talk to your potential clients" part of marketing. So I quickly threw away all those marketing-for-lawyers books and started searching for information about marketing in general.

Somehow, that search led me into the wild and crazy world we know as online marketing. Along the way, I discovered concepts like inbound marketing, content marketing, and email marketing. It made a whole hell of a lot more sense than anything in those "marketing for lawyers" books, so I started creating content to attract my ideal customers. A funny thing happened when I threw out the legal marketing books. As I niched, clarified my message, and started using inbound marketing techniques,[13] my business started to thrive.

The trouble was that even as my business was starting to thrive, I wasn't exactly happy. So I started working with a life coach.

That Freaking Life Coach Changed Everything...

My sessions with the life coach started with my relationship with my wife, my friends, my hobbies, and just about every other part of my personal life. But, at some point, we turned to my work. That's when I had one of the most important discussions of my life:

---

13. Among other things, I heard that writing a book can be great for credibility...so I wrote a real page-turner called *Patent Litigation Primer*. In case you don't know...being a "bestselling author" is not all that hard to do. That book made it to bestseller status with about twenty-five sales in the week it was released because I worked the system and got it into a super niched subcategory. Yep, I was a full-fledged online marketer who knew how to work all the angles!

Coach: "Do you like what you do for a living?"

Me: (stammering) "Uh, well…no. I don't."

Coach: "Okay, so what are we going to do about that?"[14]

Me: "I have no freaking idea."

After chatting through it a bit, she said she could see me teaching entrepreneurs about the legal stuff and suggested I'd be a natural as a guest on podcasts and radio shows. (I'm told I have a radio voice. Of course, that might just be a nice way of saying I don't have movie-star good looks.)

As a "fire, ready, aim" kind of person, I swung into action immediately. Before our next meeting two weeks later, I had hired a company to book me on forty podcasts. Mind you, I had no business—not even a plan for a business yet—but at least I was taking action.

Creating an Online Course Would Make Me Rich…Right?

It didn't take long for me to formulate my plan. I knew there were people selling "online courses," so clearly that was what I should do too. Because, y'know…why not?

My plan was simple: spend the first three quarters of 2017 building my list, getting on podcasts, and creating my course

---

14. Freaking life coaches. Sheesh. She couldn't just let me wallow in my self-pity. Instead, she demanded that I take agency over my life and make things better.

about the legal stuff for entrepreneurs…then launch that baby in November and make a shitload of money. I mean, that's what all these people online were telling me would happen. Surely, I was headed for that passive-income, living-on-a-beach, freedom lifestyle the gurus are always promising us.

Can you guess where this story is going? Do you think I got rich on that first launch?

Yeah…no. Not even close.

Throughout 2017, I spent about $50,000 on my business. During my big launch, I made precisely *one* sale, for $627. But wait, it gets worse! That customer asked for a refund on day twenty-nine of a thirty-day refund period. At the end of year one, I was in the hole $50,000.[15]

After that launch with its single sale, my life coach said it was awesome that I had made even one sale because most people don't sell anything their first time out. Um, that information would have been valuable *before* I went all in on this whole online business thing!

Business Genius from the Most Unexpected Source

To say I was in the dumps at the end of 2017 would be the understatement of the year. People who know me know that I'm not one to get depressed or really show sadness, but *whoa baby* was I feeling like shit at the end of 2017. I felt like a complete failure who had practically mortgaged his family's future on the crazy dream of building an online business.

---

15. Online entrepreneurs seem to love comparing their initial failed launches. I've yet to meet someone who was as monumentally stupid as I was, to spend *that* much on a failed year and launch. Moral of the story: don't be like Bobby!

As 2017 came to a close, I felt so shitty that I was about ready to give up this whole online thing and go back to being a boring lawyer (as much as I hated it). Fortunately, I decided to go to church rather than sulk.

On the last Sunday of the year, December 31, 2017, the pastor was talking about the power of giving and how giving changes you as a person. He didn't know it at the time, but he was speaking to my soul and giving me the will to continue. Most importantly, he was giving me the business advice I needed to hear.

Not quite grasping that the "fire, ready, aim" thing was what had gotten me into this mess, I figured that same tactic would surely be the way to get out of it! On the spot, sitting in church that Sunday, I decided that "giving" would be my word of the year for 2018.

And so I started giving—not thinking about it as a tactic, but truly giving, just to give. Giving without expectation. Giving for the joy of serving other entrepreneurs. Giving because I chose to put my audience's needs above mine. Giving because my personal values told me to be generous.

And who woulda thunk it, that sense of generosity helped me build a real freaking business. Things started to snowball in late April, when I made my first sale, and continued into May, when I made $70,000 in sales. By the end of that year, I had made a quarter of a million dollars.

As a rebel, I'm proud to say that my success had very little to do with following the "rule book" that all the online gurus were pushing. My success came from throwing that sucker out the window and building my business *my* way, based on my personal values.

Sometimes You Need Help from Tarzan

The next year, I went beyond being simply "the legal guy." People came for the legal stuff, got hooked by my emails, and then started to see me as a business mentor because of what seemed like a natural ability to connect with people.[16]

Enter Tarzan. No, not that Tarzan. My friend, and original email mentor, Tarzan Kay. On Easter Sunday, she sent me this message:

> I heard you posted something really nice about me in Amy's group—just wanted to say I'm really grateful to have a friend like you to walk this entrepreneurial road together. You're the real deal, Bobby.

> People don't talk about this much because it's not marketable, but the people I see who are successful online have an x-factor that can't be taught. You have the x-factor on steroids.

> I've been mentioning you and your emails on podcasts. Your stuff is just so good!!

> Loads of love,
> Tarzan

While I enjoyed the idea that I was special, telling a type A Harvard Law grad who naturally rebels that something "can't

---

16. My wife would assure you that I do *not* have a natural ability to connect with people. In fact, she would assure you that in real life I'm actually quite bad at connecting with people.

be taught" is like waving a red cape in front of a bull. There was only one possible response: challenge accepted!

Other people had been asking me to teach them how to do what I did, so I took Tarzan's note as a sign that it was time. I launched a membership program about how to find and cultivate raving fans, the kind of fans who will buy anything you have to sell.

Although people liked my trainings generally, they kept asking me for more about email. They wanted to know how I did *all the things* when it came to email. So I obliged them and created a signature program called BADA$$ Email Marketing, which people raved about.

But something didn't feel quite aligned for me.

My urge to *give* had become one of my core values. That's why I've given away a free privacy policy legal template for three years now, while other online lawyers charge hundreds for theirs, and it's why I've freely given of my time and knowledge in so many communities.

So, in 2020, I decided to do something that might seem utterly preposterous: I decided to just give away my email program, entirely for free. And not just my email program; my team and I created an entire free training university for online marketers, called BADA$$ Online Marketing University™ (or BOMU, as we call it).

Like I said, utterly preposterous, right? I mean, who the hell would devote his time and his team to creating course after course, giving people value *for free*, with no expectations?

A marketer would, that's who.

The launch of BOMU marked the completion of my transformation.

I am a marketer.

LAND THE PLANE, BOBBY!

About now, you might be thinking, "What the hell does any of this have to do with email?! Is Bobby just being self-indulgent?"

Well, there's a bit of self-indulgence, but my story really does have a lot to say about email marketing. The chapters here in Part I are about bringing the right frame of mind to your email marketing, and you'll see how those lessons relate to my journey.

You probably have a lot of misconceptions about how to approach email marketing. (Because most everyone does!) Here in Part I, you'll learn how to reframe your view of email marketing.

In Chapters 1 and 2, we'll dive into the *really* bad advice you're probably hearing about "marketing" and email marketing (kinda like the crappy "marketing for lawyers" advice that screwed up my journey). You'll discover what marketing is, what it isn't, and why you should focus on connecting with your audience instead of always going for a conversion. The shifts we'll talk about in these chapters are fundamental to everything that will follow because email marketing is just marketing via email. If you don't take the time to understand the core concepts of marketing, your emails will always suck.

In Chapter 3, we'll dive into the importance of having your subscribers come to see you as a friend (not some rando on the internet trying to sell them stuff). When I decided to start giving without expectation and playing the long game, everything changed for my business. And the same will be true for your email.

Finally, in Chapters 4 and 5, we'll dive into the power of bringing more of *you* to your emails. Just like I had to find the courage to stop suiting up to be me, you have to find your voice and tell your stories. This is the start of the tactical work that will build the foundation for writing emails your audience will love.

I want you to read all of Part I before moving on to Part II. Can you still become an effective email marketer, even if you skip Part I?

If it were up to me, I'd just say, "Nope, you cannot succeed without the fundamentals, so less whining, more reading." But my editor has suggested that maybe I should at least include some kind of explanation for *why* Part I is so important.

So, at my editor's insistence, here's a simple analogy to help: it's like putting together a puzzle—sure, you *might* be able to figure out where the pieces go without looking at the picture on the box, but isn't it easier if you have an idea of what the puzzle is supposed to look like?

Well, welcome to the picture on the front of the puzzle box. Part I will help you learn what you're trying to achieve with email marketing and show you how to approach it so you can have a better chance of executing the steps.

CHAPTER 1

LET'S START BY PISSING EVERYONE OFF

WHEN MY EDITOR SAW THE TITLE OF THIS CHAPTER, she naturally asked, "Err, Bobby, do you really think it's a good idea to piss everyone off this early in the book?" That might seem like a fair point, but I reminded her about those three defining elements of my voice from the Introduction. So piss people off we will. And we'll start with the craft brewers...

As someone who enjoys a good beer, you'll often find me browsing the aisles of stores that carry a wide selection of hard-to-find beers. Part of the fun is seeing the inventive names that American craft brewers have come up with. I rarely remember the names, but one will always stand out in my mind: Palate Wrecker.

It's fun to imagine the conversation at the brewery that led to them picking that name. I mean, what names did they throw out before choosing a name that basically says the beer will destroy your sense of taste? And where was the adult supervision to suggest that maybe that's *not* the best approach?

Beer has a long, proud history. It has played a pivotal role throughout time. And, until recently, brewers strove for balanced flavors. They added hops to bitter a beer to offset the sweetness of the barley, and beers were brewed extra bitter largely so they would survive long ocean voyages (which would mellow them).

Somewhere in the past couple of decades, however, a subset of American craft brewers have said "screw it" to balance in favor of extreme flavors. Rather than using hops to balance a beer, these brewers went overboard and decided that if a little is good, a lot must be better.

They are wrong. There's beauty in balance.

NOW TO PISS OFF THE EMAIL GURUS...

What's true in beer is also true in email marketing: you should be striving for a balanced approach. Just like some American craft brewers have ruined beer by overloading it with bitterness, most of the people teaching email marketing have ruined it by convincing everyone that it should be all about conversion (a.k.a. getting people to take an immediate action).

Part of the problem with the conventional wisdom about email marketing stems from the fact that the people teaching it tend to be super focused on conversions. If you survey the folks who have traditionally taught email marketing, nearly all of them fall into one of two camps.

- *The Conversion Copywriters.* Most of the people teaching email marketing in the online information business space are conversion copywriters. They are trained to get people to take action and cut their teeth writing copy for sales pages, emails, and marketing collateral used during active promotions. In other words, they focused on helping people *sell*, not market. These folks generally segued into teaching email marketing as a way to create a "scalable" product when their calendars were full and they couldn't take on more clients. Some teach email and other forms of conversion copywriting, while others choose to focus just on email.

• *The Funnel Strategists.* The other group is made up of people who are uber-focused on sales funnels. They may have started by creating their own sales funnels or by consulting with clients on how to design the *best* sales funnel possible. They've generally never met a sale, upsell, downsell, left sell, right sell, dark sell, or light sell that they don't love.[17]

Between these two camps, you can pretty much guess that the email marketing teachers are like the proverbial person with a hammer…they're always in search of a nail.

Conversion copywriters and funnel strategists are trained to do something very specific: make the sale!

I'm here to not-so-humbly suggest that selling and conversions actually should *not* be the focus of everything you do with your email marketing…or even your marketing more generally. To be clear, I'm all for selling, but we need balance.

---

17. Okay, I made up a few of those "sells," but there's probably someone out there trying to figure out how to do a dark sell right now!

IT'S NOT JUST EMAIL...EVERYTHING YOU THINK YOU KNOW ABOUT MARKETING IS PROBABLY WRONG

Most of the conventional wisdom about email is dead wrong, but email isn't the problem. The problem is that "email marketing" is just one form of marketing, and you've been learning marketing from people who don't seem to know what that word actually means.[18]

The online marketing industry has a pervasive problem. The people teaching marketing in the space tend to think of marketing as a synonym for advertising and/or selling. As a result, we've been taught to focus (almost exclusively) on what is called "direct-response marketing." Direct-response marketing is just a fancy phrase to capture any type of marketing that is *conversion* focused. With direct-response, you're after an immediate action from your prospect—whether it's a click, a form sign up, or a sale.

But, err, direct-response marketing is only one *very* small part of marketing. Given that you've probably been learning email marketing from people who don't really understand marketing, it's no wonder email marketing hasn't worked for you. Your emails aren't going to work until you learn a thing or two about marketing.

But what the hell *is* marketing anyway? What are the basic concepts you need to know?

The American Marketing Association defines marketing as "the activity, set of institutions, and processes for creating, communicating, delivering, and exchanging offerings that have value for customers, clients, partners, and society at large."

---

18. That should check the "marketing gurus" and everyone who loves them off my list of people to piss off today! Wonder who's next???

The Princess Bride

Whenever I hear someone in the online space say the word "marketing," I can't help but think of *The Princess Bride*. Suddenly, I am the Inigo Montoya to the online gurus' Vizzini: "You keep using that word. I do not think it means what you think it means."

That's way too many fancy words for my taste. Hell, my lawyer friends would probably be jealous at how "legalese-y" the AMA made that sound. I tend to use penny and nickel words, so here's how I describe marketing: marketing is about offering the right product to the right person at the right time, with the right message.

(And, by the way, that means right for *them*, not for *me* or *you*. Marketing is about serving your audience, not about what you want or need as the marketer.)

Before we dig deeper into what exactly all those "rights" mean, it's time for a stroll down marketing's memory lane.

A BRIEF (NON-BORING) HISTORY OF MARKETING

Historically, there have been—depending on who you ask—either four or five "concepts" of marketing.

Marketing started with the *production concept*, which basically says people want shit to be cheap and readily available. Under this theory, your goal is to make your product as efficiently as possible so you can make it as cheap as possible. This continues to be the standard idea of marketing for commodities and raw materials (like cotton).

Some people think of the second concept of marketing as the *product concept*, which went the other way and said that people want products to be better and fancier. This concept led to the "build a better mousetrap" approach, where people were adding bells and whistles to everything. The problem with this concept is that, at some level, you don't need everything to be better. At some point, you just need it to be *good enough*.

Then came the *selling concept* of marketing, which was prominent throughout the 1950s and early 1960s. This concept was based on the notion that there won't be enough natural demand for a product, so your job as marketer is to create demand for your product. Professional marketers figured out that this concept is dumb because trying to create demand is a fool's errand. And it turns you into the worst of the pushy salespeople we all detest. That is *not* a good way to create happy, long-term customers.

In the 1960s, professional marketers transitioned to the *marketing concept*,[19] which is best described as "sense and react" marketing. Rather than trying to create demand, your job as a marketer is to sense the market demand and create a product to meet that demand. In other words, marketing is about listening to your audience and creating solutions to the problems they already have (and that they are looking for solutions to!).

Professional marketers have moved past even that concept to an approach known either as *holistic marketing* or *relationship marketing*. As you can probably guess, this concept emphasizes viewing marketing as a whole and building relationships. It's

---

19. Next on the "to piss off" list are the marketing academics. They clearly need to hire some *actual* marketers to help them name stuff because, come *on*…"the marketing concept of marketing" is the most uninspired name ever!

about your relationships with your customers, your peers, your team, and the different parts of your market. And this concept goes even further, noting that we, as marketers, should consider the impact we are having on the world at large. That's why we now see companies like Tom's giving away a pair of shoes with every pair you buy or Ben and Jerry's having a social aspect from the start. Taking a stand for what you believe is right is now the norm, not the exception.

In today's world, a professional marketer learns to listen—to sense and react—but also to build relationships, to see the connections between everyone involved in those relationships, and to be willing to take a stand for the things they believe in.

ONLINE MARKETERS MISSED THE MEMO

Unfortunately, most of the people teaching email marketing (and a lot of the people who claim to teach about anything related to online marketing) aren't actually teaching marketing. At least, they aren't teaching *modern* marketing. It's almost like they got their hands on a DeLorean and, instead of going into the future to get a sports almanac, they went back to 1955 to get their hands on a marketing book!

Oh wait…that's kinda what happened.

Most people in the online marketing world are using tactics from a direct-response marketing playbook. No, seriously, there is a playbook. If you hang out among people who really geek out on messaging and copywriting in the online space, you are bound to hear them talk about a book written in the 1960s called *Breakthrough Advertising*.

As far as it goes, *Breakthrough Advertising* is a great book. Understanding its concepts will help you write amazing sales copy. That book was written by a copywriter who got exactly *one chance* to convince someone to buy. He wrote ads to be published around the country that were intended to get people to call (or write) to buy something that they had never heard of before seeing the ad. In that context, direct-response marketing is really the *only* option.

The trouble is that people somehow mistook a book about a particular kind of advertising as covering *everything we need to know* about marketing! So they ended up thinking that marketing and direct-response marketing are one and the same. Ultimately, they're stuck in the antiquated selling concept of marketing. To them, marketing is all about selling.

While selling is part of marketing, it's only one very small piece of the puzzle. Don't believe me? Here's a challenge for you: check out any master's program in marketing and see how many of those courses are about selling.

This just in: my editor says I should *not* tell you to put this book down to go do research.[20] I told her that you've already bought the damn book and, according to what I've learned from the online marketing crew, that's all that really matters (cause, you know, you gave me your money already!). She says I should want you to actually read this thing and is worried that my witty repartee isn't good enough to guarantee that you'll come back.

Fine. We'll do it her way!

---

20. If you actually did the research, though, you'd find that these programs don't focus on selling or direct-response marketing. Nope. In fact, most master's programs in marketing that I've looked at include precisely *zero* courses on sales.

How about you listen to one of the most well-known business thinkers, Peter Drucker. He said this about the relationship between sales and marketing:

> There will always, one can assume, be a need for some selling. But the aim of marketing is to make selling superfluous. The aim of marketing is to know and understand the customer so well that the product or service fits him and sells itself. Ideally, marketing should result in a customer who is ready to buy. All that should be needed then is to make the product or service available.[21]

In other words, effective marketing is supposed to be about eliminating the need for selling altogether. While it doesn't always work out *that* easily, effective marketing is about making sales easier.

To be clear: selling isn't bad, and there's nothing wrong with being tactical or having a sales strategy. The problem comes in mistaking a *sales* strategy for a *marketing* strategy. With that approach, you are constantly on a treadmill. When you stop selling, stop asking for a response, you stop getting it. That focus on selling, to the exclusion of other marketing principles, means that those people haven't taken the time to build goodwill or to become someone their subscribers know, like, and trust—and without that reputation, the sales treadmill is likely to buck them off when it comes to an abrupt stop.

21. Peter Drucker, *Management: Tasks, Responsibilities, Practices* (New York: Harper and Row, 1973), 64–65. (Hey, look, a real footnote! Don't worry, we'll get back to the nonsense footnotes in no time.)

SELLING IS *NOT* SERVICE...MARKETING IS

While we're on the subject of the difference between marketing and selling, we've got to talk about one of the biggest misconceptions floating around the online marketing world: the idea that "selling is service." If you've been around for a while, I'm guessing you've heard that once or twice as people tell you not to feel bad about asking for the sale. Hell, I used to perpetuate that misconception by saying, "Selling is a service when it's done right."

But I was wrong. Dead wrong.

Pretty much *by definition*, selling is *not* service. Selling is about your needs as the seller, not your audience's needs. But don't just take my word for it; here's how a Harvard Business School professor described the difference between marketing and selling:

> Selling focuses on the needs of the seller; marketing on the needs of the buyer. Selling is preoccupied with the seller's need to convert his product into cash; marketing with the idea of satisfying the needs of the customer by means of the product and the whole cluster of things associated with creating, delivering, and finally consuming it.[22]

Selling is, by nature, about your needs. Service, on the other hand, is about other people's needs. Ergo,[23] selling is not about

---

22. Theodore Levitt, "Marketing Myopia," *Harvard Business Review* (July-August 1960): 50. (See, I wasn't making shit up when I said that professional marketers started to move away from the "selling concept" in the early 1960s. Damn, it's like I actually know what I'm talking about! Where is the shrug emoji when I need it?!)

23. Look Mom...a fancy logic word!

service, no matter how many times your coach has you repeat that as a mantra or business affirmation.[24]

Marketing, on the other hand, is *all* about service. It is relentlessly interested in the needs of the buyer. Marketing is, above all else, about putting your potential customers' needs first and foremost and serving the heck out of them. Marketing is about being a serve-first entrepreneur. And we're not talking about the lip-service version of being serve-first that so many entrepreneurs profess but don't actually practice.

When you create the *right* offer and put it in front of the *right* person at the *right* time with the *right* message, you don't have to sell. Marketing is how you make sales without selling. It's how you make sales through service. It's how you make sales almost as if by magic.

But it's not magic. It's marketing.

Choosing to market rather than sell is about making a series of choices, including:

- *You over Me*. Marketers don't ask what will make them the most money. They ask how they can best serve the needs of their customers. In a mind-bending way, focusing on service rather than making money tends to make you more money in the long term. Just as importantly, it makes it pretty stinking easy to make decisions. When facing a choice, you always revert to a single question: How can I best serve my audience?

---

24. There go the coaches! Is there really anyone left for me to piss off???

- *Giving over Taking.* Marketers don't view transactions as a zero-sum game where they are trying to get every last dollar for themselves. They strive to *always* leave every person better than when they entered the relationship. In other words, they seek to find ways that they can truly benefit their customers.

- *People over Transactions.* Marketers don't think of people simply as a wallet that might buy something. Instead, they think of people as, you know, *human freaking beings.* (Crazy idea, I know.) They happily serve their people, even those who might never buy, and they most definitely don't complain about "freebie seekers" on their lists.

- *Passion over Profits.* Marketers tend to have a passion for the people they serve and for the particular way they serve them. That passion (not the endless pursuit of profits) is what motivates them to put in the work to serve their people.

- *Long Term over Short Term.* Marketers focus on what will build their brand and business over years and decades, not days and months. While sellers focus on making every last sale, regardless of what's right for the customer, marketers recognize that the better course is to focus on what is best for the customer over the long term (even if that means telling them not to buy right now).

- *Warm Audiences over Cold Leads.* Marketers don't expect to bring people into a funnel and have money magically appear. Instead, they focus on building a connection with people to warm them up, and they understand that sales come more organically after a significant journey with the customer. To put it another way, they focus on sales coming from their warm audience, *not* expecting people to come into their world cold and buy.

Reading that list may have you saying, "Holy crap, Bobby, marketing sounds hard!" And you would be right. Marketing is most definitely not easy. But nothing worth doing is. Marketing is about making an investment in your business that will bring returns long into the future.

MARKETING IS A LEAP OF FAITH

If I haven't scared you away yet, this just might do it. Marketing, unlike selling, is most definitely not about a direct, immediate return on investment.

Being a marketer, not a seller, requires a leap of faith. It means being willing to spend time, effort, and money on marketing efforts that do *not* have a direct response. It means being willing to spend money on ads that won't result in a sale over the short term because you know that investment in your business will pay off in the long run.

That's what Apple does. That's what Coca-Cola does. Hell, that's what every brand you know and love does.

I get it; you're probably objecting to those comparisons based on a line we've all been fed by the conventional wisdom in the online space: "But online businesses are different, so the rules that work for big brands just don't apply to us!"

Really? Why? No one has been able to give me a legitimate reason why we are different in a way that matters. In fact, the differences tend to prove that we should focus even *more* on brand-building marketing. I mean, we are, after all, companies who are driven more by personality and a personal connection to the founder than big companies.

But my own profit and loss statements prove the point. As of the time I'm writing this book, right around 65 percent of the sales of my signature legal offer (which costs $997) come purely from brand awareness. No funnel. No ad. No call to action. Buyers come as if by magic…but my analytics tell me a good chunk of them searched "Bobby Klinck legal templates" and then bought.

Can I track those sales to a particular dollar I spent on advertising? Nope.

Can I track those sales to any particular marketing initiative? Nope.

Can I track those sales to a particular *thing* I did? Nope.

As scary as it may sound…that's marketing.

Although it feels like a frightening leap of faith, the reality is that the marketing approach is less risky than the alternative. While you can't track results directly to a single action, marketing has stood the test of time. Building brand awareness and good-will are proven strategies. The leap of faith isn't about forgoing strategy or tactics; it's about choosing the strategy that has been proven to lead to long-term success.

Am I saying you should ditch all your direct-response efforts, funnels, and sales strategies? Of course not. We run conversion ads all the time, to get people onto my email list and when we run promotions. But the bulk of our focus is on marketing efforts (whether advertising or otherwise) that are about positioning the brand so that people will come and buy…as if by magic.

And if you're asking my opinion—which you kind of are, by reading this book—I think that's how you should approach your marketing too.

BUILD A BRAND; DON'T BUY LOTTERY TICKETS

Candidly, a big part of the problem with entrepreneurship is that we've lionized the people who have gone all in, taken huge risks, and had it pay off. But that's like seeing that someone won the lottery and concluding that sinking your life savings into lottery tickets is a solid financial plan.[25] The reality is that the direct-response, selling-heavy approach so many people are pushing you to use amounts to this same type of all-or-nothing approach.

That approach does not work for the vast majority of people who try it. Instead of hitting it big, they end up broke, convinced they are a failure, and searching for a job they don't really want because they're made to feel entrepreneurship just isn't for them.

Don't think I'm throwing stones here—that's the point I was at, at the end of 2017. Had I not thrown out the online marketing rulebook and started focusing on giving, connecting, and building brand awareness, I would have been one of those people who end up chewed up and spit out by this industry.

Hearing that you probably can't get rich with the "easy button" approach is a downer, I know! People don't want to hear

---

25. Since I'm a lawyer and don't want to get my ass sued, let me be 100 percent clear. Do not, I repeat, *do not*, sink your life savings into lottery tickets.

this, but it's the truth. If you want to build a successful business, you've got to be willing to live with the "hard button." You could keep chasing secrets, hoping to find the unicorn solution, but you'll be looking for a long time.

Marketing is an art as much as it's a science. It's something you have to work at and practice. You need to get to the point where you're proficient and understand the principles so you can figure it out yourself. If you're just trying to check all the boxes and do what you're told you *should* do, it's not going to work.

It all comes down to this: if you want a business that's going to be here ten years from now—or five years from now or, hell, a year from now—you have to be a marketer, not a salesperson.

BRINGING IT ALL BACK TO EMAIL

So what the hell does all of this have to do with email anyway? Well, how about we start with the obvious: it's called email *marketing*, not email *selling*. I was tempted to leave it at that, but again my editor says that maybe explaining a bit more would help, so here goes.

The focus on sales-heavy, direct-response marketing isn't just a problem with how people advertise and show up on the front end to cold audiences. It has infected the way people approach email marketing too. Because we've been so trained to think in terms of "getting the click" and immediate return on investment, we fixate on the wrong things. Every email is overly tactical, which sucks for you as the person writing it and *extra* sucks for the people who are supposed to be reading it.

As an email marketer, you probably feel pressure to write the *perfect* email each week, which puts an insane amount of pressure on you. That's why that blinking cursor can feel like it's mocking you. Imagine how freeing it would feel and how much easier and more fun writing emails could be if you thought of them simply as a way to connect with your subscribers as people. No special tactics. No pressure to get the click. No need to measure anything, really.

And think about it from the perspective of your subscribers. Do you think they like that every email they get from you has "an angle"? Trust me; they can see what you're up to. When your emails feel like a sales pitch, even if only for a click, people stop paying attention because nobody likes being sold to.

So your mission, should you choose to accept it, is to stop trying to constantly sell via email and instead start marketing via email. In the following chapters, we'll talk about exactly how to do that in greater detail.

And now that I've thoroughly pissed everyone off, it's time to get specific and tell you who *really* ruined email marketing!

CHAPTER 2

JUST DO THE DAMN DISHES

REMEMBER THAT LIFE COACH I MENTIONED IN THE introduction to Part I? She didn't just play a pivotal role in my entrepreneurial journey. Working with her was also the best thing I ever did to improve my relationship with my wife. The *one* conversation that I'll always remember was about doing the dishes. The conversation went something like this:

"Do you know your wife's love language?"

"Yep. Acts of service."

"What is the one thing you could do to help her that would make her happiest?"

"Washing the dishes, I guess."

"When's the last time you washed the dishes *just because*…not hoping that she would do something for you in return?"

"I can't remember. It's been a long time."

"How about you just do the damn dishes tonight?"

That conversation was an aha moment for me. Too much of what was happening in my relationships with other people was a transaction. I was doing something hoping to get something that I wanted in return.

My coach was encouraging me to quit thinking transactionally and just serve without expectation. Little did I know that she was teaching me to be a marketer without even meaning to!

MARKETING IS ABOUT RELATIONSHIPS

My life coach was teaching me about marketing because effective marketing is all about *relationships*.

The standard approach to email marketing ignores one of the most important concepts of marketing: the importance of building the know, like, and trust factor. These days, getting people to agree on *anything* is next to impossible, but if you challenged me to come up with one pretty universally accepted principle among marketers, it would be that people want to buy from people they know, like, and trust.

The know, like, and trust factor is even *more important* for the typical online brand, which is selling information, services, or some form of expertise. A knowledge brand cannot survive without building authority (trust) and connection (know and like). People aren't going to buy from you if any of these components are missing! Your relationship with the people in your audience will be one of the most important factors to your success. When you take the time to build those relationships through consistent email marketing campaigns, the results are pretty magical.

I experienced the power of building the know, like, and trust factor when I ran a "founding member" launch to enter the business coaching space. Up to that point, I had simply been the legal guy. The idea of launching a business-focused membership scared the living shit out of me, but I hit send on an email inviting my list to join my new membership with little more than a vision. The response was amazing because I had built a relationship that made them trust me.

I had no real idea what I was going to say in my *second* invite email…that is, until someone responded to my first email with her view on whether it was risky to trust me. At that point, the second email wrote itself:

From: Bobby Klinck

Date: May 14, 2019

Subject: "Taking a chance on Bobby… doesn't feel so risky :)"

Yesterday, I told you that I've decided to launch a membership site to help entrepreneurs create their tribes of raving fans.

My goal is to help you find, attract, and connect with your 1000 true fans (or maybe even more!!!).

(continued on page 34)

(continued from page 33)

Since you're someone who has supported me by grabbing my signature legal product, I would love for you to become a founding member for a one-time payment of $297.

I notice you opened yesterdays email but haven't joined yet...

I get that joining a membership that hasn't been created yet based on a vision may seem risky.

I mean... you'd be betting on me.

Betting that I'm going to overdeliver value when it comes to this membership.

I'm hoping that from knowing me, you've got a sense that betting on me to overdeliver isn't exactly going out on a limb.

That's why I loved it when one person who joined yesterday said:

"Taking a chance on Bobby... doesn't feel so risky :)"

My goal is ALWAYS to overdeliver, so it's good to hear that people don't really feel like betting on me is a risk!

Here's hoping you have the same feeling.

If so, you can join the my new membership as a founding member by clicking here. (As a quick reminder, the membership will launch on June 17, but to become a founding member for just $297 you have to join today.)

If you've decided that my new membership isn't for you, that's 100% cool with me (and you can quit reading...).

But I want to make damn sure that you can make a decision one way or the other, so I'm here to answer any questions you have.

(continued on page 35)

(continued from page 34)

I would hate for you to miss this opportunity because I didn't address something you need answered.

So, if you have questions, just HIT REPLY and ask.

Or better yet, send me a text at (202) XXX-XXXX.

Yep, that's my personal cell number.

I've got a few things going on today (the dog has to go to the vet and the 'rents are leaving after a week-long stay), but I'll find time to answer any questions you have.

And if we need to jump on the phone for a quick chat, I'm happy to do it.

My goal isn't to sell you on something you don't need... I want to help you make the best decision for you and your business.

As a quick reminder, this offer is going away at midnight tonight, so if you are at all interested... reach out!

Talk later.

Bobby

My membership invite was a big ask. It required people to trust that I would deliver. I ended up having forty-five people join as founding members, without anything more than that vision, because I had spent the time to build the know, like, and trust factor.

None of that would have happened if I had approached email as transactional and all about conversion.

IF YOU'RE FOCUSED ON OPEN RATES AND CLICK-THROUGH RATES... YOU'RE DOING IT WRONG!

One of the biggest symptoms of the transaction focus for email is the incessant talk about open rates and click-through rates as a gauge of our success with email. If you spend more than about twelve seconds in a group of online marketers, you're bound to hear questions like:

> "What are typical open rates for your newsletters?"
> "My click-through rate is 5 percent. Is that good?"
> "My email open rate is 57 percent. Should I be worried?"[26]

People get *so fixated* on these numbers that they engineer everything in their emails around increasing the open rates and click-through rates.[27] Case in point: I'm in an online entrepreneur group where a woman posted a comment about how she has a 50 percent open rate with a list that was in the multiple thousands. Typically, once your list is at that level, you can expect a 20 percent to 30 percent open rate, if you do really well. (Just to give you a general sense, I tend to get somewhere between 30 percent and 35 percent open rates.) So how was her rate at a whopping 50 percent?

People started asking her, "Wow, how are you getting such amazing open rates?" She explained that she is a web developer

---

26. No, not a typo...humblebragging is alive and well online.

27. As I'm finalizing edits to this book, Apple is rolling out iOS 15. This update will make open rates useless. Without boring you with the details, every email to a subscriber who uses the native Apple mail app will show up in your email system as having been opened regardless of whether the person actually opened the email. Cool, huh? I mean, it might feel awesome to see 60 percent open rates, but it will tell you nothing.

who helps other web developers learn how to code and build websites. She then explained that *every* email includes a different piece of CSS code, which her subscribers could use to build websites for their clients.[28]

Suddenly, it all made sense: people were opening her emails because it was transactional. It was an exchange. They knew that in each email, they would get something they could copy and paste into a library of code somewhere that they could use in their business.

Here's the kicker, though…even with her very high open rates, it turned out that she was struggling to get people to buy from her! The problem was that she was so focused on getting opens that she wasn't doing anything to build a connection or to cultivate a relationship with people who might buy down the road. These people weren't opening the email to get to know her. They were just opening it to get the code. Any email that didn't include a snippet of code was ignored because people were just there for the free stuff.

Bobby's Swift Kick in the Ass

Now, do *not* take what I just said to suggest that I think giving stuff away for free is a bad thing! To the contrary, one of my core values is to be a radical giver, which means people tend to know me as that wacky guy on the internet who just gives all his stuff away for free. But being a radical giver is about a mindset, not a tactic. You're not giving to get something in return or because

---

28. If you don't know what CSS code is, you're lucky.

you expect reciprocity (even if that's just expecting an "open"). You're giving because you are a giver and you want to give for giving's sake without any other expectation.

To understand how to give the right way, every business owner should read *The Go-Giver* by Bob Burg and John David Mann. Their book reflects the ultimate truth that establishing *giving* as a way of life is one of the most powerful shifts you can make.

You can't really blame this woman for chasing open rates because she had almost certainly been taught that she should measure the success of her email marketing by looking at stats like open rates and click-through rates.

The reality is that those stats are pretty meaningless. After all, what does an open mean? Yes, people have to open my email in order to read it. But that doesn't measure whether they read the email, or enjoyed it, or got something out of it. It just measures whether or not they opened it, *even if they deleted it immediately after*. An open is basically a "meh" reaction.

Even click-through rates are deceiving. The woman giving CSS code out like candy could've generated sky-high click-through rates by forcing subscribers to click through to a web page to grab the code. But would that have been a sign that her audience was engaged and more likely to buy? Nope. And it sure as hell wouldn't have been the best way to serve her audience.

Numbers may not lie…but they sure as hell don't tell you the whole story.

SCREW CONVERSION…I WANT CONVERSATIONS

Now, I'd like to tell you that I'm a freaking genius and have always known that we should focus on connection instead of conversion. But that whole "thou shalt not lie" thing throws a wrench into that plan. As with many things in my life, I stumbled into this knowledge through sheer luck. Because I'm loquacious,[29] I chose a podcast as my primary form of content, which by nature means I'm unlikely to have high click-through rates on my weekly emails.

When people listen to podcasts, they don't typically click the link in an email to go to a website and listen. Instead, they listen in Stitcher or Apple Podcasts or Spotify or one of the dozens of other podcast players. Since people don't click to listen, I never worry about click-through rates. In fact, I'd think it was kind of weird if a bunch of people *were* clicking on the podcast link from my emails. I'd be asking, "Don't you know about all these services you can use to listen to podcasts?"

What I stumbled upon because I was a podcaster applies equally no matter what form of content you create. There is power in ignoring click-through rates. Instead of sabotaging my efforts by focusing on getting those clicks, I was able to focus on being *relational*, not transactional. My goal became getting engagement.

So if opens and clicks aren't the goal for engagement, then what is?

Simple: replies.

I care more about people clicking reply and responding to me than I care about them clicking on anything else…but I rarely

---

29. Look Mom, an SAT word!

ask people to respond. When you constantly focus on building connection, you don't have to ask for replies. People just tend to feel compelled to respond.

While I now have a bunch of people who reply quite regularly (more on how to get that to happen in a bit), the first time someone replies almost always starts the same way: "I never respond to these types of emails, but..." There is gold in that! Think about what that means. They're getting hundreds, if not thousands, of emails from lists, and they've *never* responded, but they felt compelled to respond to mine. Either I've pulled the ultimate Jedi mind trick (unlikely) or I have connected with them at a deep level (yeah, it's probably that).

Since some of you are just here for the money, rest assured that the people you connect with become the people who don't even have to think twice about buying from you.

But wait...there's more!

Getting replies also gives you the chance to have a conversation. That should have you jumping for joy because those conversations are where the real magic happens. If you take the time to engage with those people (you know, hit reply yourself!), you'll often get to hear your audience describe their struggles and goals in *their own words.*

Screw pictures; those words are priceless. Because when you have their words, you can use their language in marketing communication, ads, and sales pages. You can craft copy and messaging that makes them feel like you actually "get" them. Opens and clicks won't get you that...but listening (read: connecting!) will. Beyond the words themselves, you'll learn what your people are really struggling with, what they've already tried, and why it didn't work for them.

For every person who did reply, there are probably hundreds (or even thousands or tens of thousands, depending on the size of your list) who didn't reply but are thinking and feeling the same things as the people who did.

I'll take one conversation over a high click-through rate any day of the week and twice on Sunday.

One caveat: I'm not suggesting that you think of your email as a way to always be conducting market research. In other words, don't constantly ask questions like "If I were going to create something about X, what would you want me to say?" Those emails have their place, and you might get some responses that way. But those guided responses aren't worth nearly as much as the natural responses you get when people reply without you asking. You'll find that your best "market research" is not in asking for replies. Instead, the best market research comes from building relationships and learning organically.

One further piece of guidance: make sure the email comes from you. Guess what will kill engagement faster than boring emails? If your audience sees your emails coming from support@yourdomain.com or info@whateveryourbusinessiscalled.org. The "from" should be your name and the replies should come to your inbox.

Additionally, the length and depth of your reply should match the length and depth of theirs. If someone writes, "Hey, great email," then you can just respond, "Hey, thanks!" You might even ask, "What'd you like about it?" But if someone writes a multi-paragraph response, take the time to really read it and respond with a similarly well thought-out answer.

Taking the time to engage with people who do reply is how you'll go from occasional responses to cultivating a whole list of people who reply regularly. By responding when they click reply, you are rewarding them for taking the action you want. Most people will be amazed that you respond. Heck, they probably think their reply might go to someone on your team, but it's probably not going to be read by *you*. When you personally respond, they're blown away. You are taking the time to read their emails and reply back to them. You respect them as people, as your friends, and they took the time to give you a story or some information, so you give that back when you respond.

Those people become die-hard fans. They become your brand advocates. The people telling everyone else to get their asses on your list and buy your shit. But that only happens if you're willing to engage.

If they're not hitting reply, you can't start the conversation. So how about focusing on getting replies, mmmkay?

IS IT RELATABLE? THAT'S DEBATABLE

If I haven't completely pissed off the conversion-centered folks, here comes the statement that'll do it: *do not track reply statistics!*

Wait, what? I tell you that your goal should be to get replies, but now I'm telling you not to track that as a statistic? The folks who think numbers tell them everything in their business are either pulling their hair out or yelling at me right now.[30]

Here's my logic. When you start tracking numbers, you'll naturally fixate on them. Guess what that leads to? You'll start chasing some arbitrary numbers by forcing it. You'll start asking

---

30. My long-suffering number two, Katie, has surely stopped reading by now…but she would definitely be pulling her hair out at this comment.

for replies or coming up with some other random artificial trick to increase engagement. That defeats the purpose.

Now, because you're almost certainly going to ignore my advice and insist on knowing how many replies you should be getting, let's set some expectations. If you have a list of a hundred people, you're probably not going to get regular replies. You'll get them every once in a while, but as your list grows, you'll start to see them more consistently, and they'll increase as you continue to engage with your people. At this point, I get replies to nearly every email I send but have no idea how many.

The way to get replies is to just be yourself and tell stories that let people into your life. In Chapter 6 and again in Part II, we'll look at how to structure emails. The key to engagement is in finding the right kinds of stories to tell. You want people to be able to relate to your stories. That means you should *not* be telling stories that are completely *unrelatable* to your average reader. For example, I don't tell many stories about Harvard Law School (except to poke fun) or the cases I worked on where we were fighting about hundreds of millions or billions of dollars.[31] That's just not the world that the people I serve would relate to.

Instead, I tend to choose stories that make fun of me and my crazy antics because everyone can relate to that *one* friend. You may not know exactly how an email will be relatable at first, but you'll get a feel in time.

One of my classic emails recounted my crowning moment as a debater in high school. I could explain the email, but that would be silly. Why don't you just read it?

---

31. Yeah, I was once involved in a case that ended up in a $1.4 billion judgment. If only that had been a contingency fee case where I represented the plaintiff! Alas, I'm not rolling in that kind of money over here.

From: Bobby Klinck

Date: September 11, 2018

Subject: I may have peaked as a high school senior...

Hey Jillian,

This week's episode of the Online Genius Podcast is all about dealing with the mental baggage that is getting in the way of your success.

But before we get to that, I want to tell you about how I may have peaked as a high school debater...

In high school, I was on the debate team, which I loved. As much as I loved debate, there was one thing that was a real problem for me...

My debate coach always made us compete in other events too. Most of the time, these other events did not go well...

...Except for the one time when he entered us into this crazy event called "impromptu speaking."

Here's the gist... you walk into a room and randomly pick a slip of paper with a topic, prepare for a few minutes, and then give a 5-10 minute speech.

The speech is supposed to be organized (as if you are making a persuasive argument) but also funny. As a debater, organized was in my wheelhouse... but funny, not so much.

"What the hell am I going to do with this topic?!?!"

I walked into the room and picked my the piece of paper with the topic and looked down to see this:

(continued on page 45)

(continued from page 44)

If you could give yourself any nickname, what would it be and why?

I was perplexed… I mean, how the hell was I going to give a funny but organized speech about that?!?

…And then I looked out the window in the door and saw my friend Brandon.

Here's a picture of me and the debate team. Brandon is the guy in the leather jacket in front with me (yep, that's me in the blue and red shirt sporting my ponytail!):

Suddenly I remembered how Brandon had been razzing me earlier that day…

Pretty much the whole day, Brandon had been making fun of my ego… Back then, I was kind of known for being a bit, shall we say, self-assured.

That was my lightbulb moment, and I mapped out my speech in my head in about 30 seconds. And then it was time to start, so I opened with this:

(continued on page 46)

(continued from page 45)

If I had to give myself a nickname, it would be Goe... because that's one after God in the alphabet.

That's right, I was going to OWN it. I wasn't going to run from my flaw or pretend it wasn't there... I was going to freaking embrace it!

My first two points were quite cogent. I spent about four minutes explaining that I was good at everything and that everybody loved me.

At that point in the speech, I was not exactly #winning... the judge had chuckled at the first line, but he didn't seem all that amused with my cogent arguments about how wonderful I was. Go figure!

Luckily, I knew the best was yet to come. This was how I started my final point:

Third, and honestly most importantly ... I'm VERY humble.

When I delivered that line, the judge literally (yes, I actually mean literally) fell out of his chair laughing.

That was my mic drop moment...

As a debater, a law student, a lawyer, and an entrepreneur, I've given A LOT of speeches, but none as good as that one. So, yeah, I may have peaked in my speaking career as a senior in high school.

That brings me back to this week's podcast episode...

In **this week's episode of The Online Genius Podcast**, I interview Lisa Carpenter.

Lisa helps high achieving entrepreneurs own their personal power and establish value-based boundaries with her Full Frontal Living™ approach. Lisa encourages us to stop trying to "do" our way to success and empowers us to stay present to what we're feeling and how we're showing up in all areas of our life.

(continued on page 47)

(continued from page 46)

During the interview, Lisa talked about how too many of us refuse to face our issues and how this ends up hurting us.

That's why I shared my "Goe" story. It's a comical example of facing some baggage and thriving as a result. We could all stand to do that more in every part of our lives, even when it isn't quite as much fun as giving a funny speech...

Lisa shared some great wisdom that can help you do just that. But she also talked about a lot of other great stuff, including:

- The common problem that high achievers face.

- What tends to be the root problem for workaholics.

- How to begin confronting your feelings to deal with the underlying issues.

- What her Full Frontal Living™ message is all about.

- The reason high achievers have trouble making time for self-care.

- How high achievers can get into the practice of making self-care a non-negotiable.

- A simple trick to quiet your mind.

It is a really great interview.

Click here to give the episode a listen.

Talk later.

Bobby

(continued on page 48)

(continued from page 47)

P.S. The backstory of Brandon making fun of me was that although I was cocky as a debater, it wasn't exactly unfounded. During my senior year, I probably won about 75% of the tournaments we went to, and I ultimately won the Texas state championship in debate. But here's the funny thing, I don't remember a single debate or even a single argument I made during my debating career. But I sure a shit remember the time I made a judge fall out of his chair laughing because I wasn't afraid to make fun of myself a little bit. I try to remember that these days… and it helps me to avoid taking myself too seriously.

I thought the email had a funny story and that people could relate to the self-deprecating humor. Little did I know that someone in my audience would relate more directly. After reading this email, someone responded to tell me that she had to do that same event! It was so weird and funny—in my entire debate career, I had only seen this event once, and yet someone in my audience had the same experience.   *e.g. the old carpe*

You never know what's going to connect, and you can't plan that kind of relatability or connection. But now when that woman thinks of me, I'm that guy who did that same wacky speaking event as she did. Now I've become that person who is related to something else in her life, something personal for her.

JUST DO THE DAMN DISHES

Ultimately, the trouble with the normal approach to email marketing is that the constant focus on conversions turns everything into a transaction. And that approach won't work over the long haul.

This is something that I immediately got when my life coach and I had that discussion about doing the dishes. The trouble is that we too often ignore solid lessons from our personal relationships that apply to building a business.

If we know that the transactional approach *doesn't* work in our personal relationships, why the hell would we think that being purely transactional would work in business?

In other words, you have to stop looking at your business (and email) through the eyes of a conversion copywriter and start seeing it through the eyes of a loving spouse. Build relationships and forget about the transactions.

Choosing to just do the damn dishes isn't easy, but it gets easier with practice. You'll get better at it, and you'll get to the point where your people are responding because you've given them so much and they want to give you something too. A story, feedback, or just a moment of their time to say, "Thanks" or "That was funny."

Now that I've told you how to improve your marriage, it's time to talk about making some new friends. We'll look at how to do that in the next chapter—oh yeah…and lice; we can't forget about the lice!

CHAPTER 3

LICE REMEDIES GALORE

IN SEPTEMBER 2019, my daughter had just started kindergarten, and I was enjoying having the house all to myself for a full day. I planned to get so much done…until I got an email from her school with a one-word subject line: "LICE."

The rest of my day became a journey into the depths of the internets to figure out how to make damn sure she didn't bring lice into my house—without having to shave her head or burn all her stuff (which my wife stubbornly refused to even consider).

That escapade took up my entire day and ended up being the subject of the email I sent out the following day:

From: Bobby Klinck

Date: September 6, 2019

Subject: My 4-hour lice-capade...

Wednesday was supposed to be one of those crazy mega batching days...

...my ring light was full blast, my mic was set up, my makeup was on, the shot list was ready...

I was gonna crank through a half dozen videos (even had multiple shirts picked out!).

And then midway through the second video, I got an urgent email with a single word subject line:

"LICE!"

It was a note from my daughter's kindergarten teacher to tell us that there was a "confirmed" case of lice in the class.

And with that the video shoot went out the window...

Making sure my daughter (and my house!!!) stayed lice-free became my A1 Sauce.

For some reason, my wife insisted that shaving my daughter's head and burning the clothes she was wearing wasn't an option. 🙍‍♂️

So... I had to find a different solution.

I turned to the book of face, solicited opinions from friends, scoured the internets, ordered way too much from Amazon, and headed to my neighborhood CVS for an immediate fix.

(continued on page 53)

(continued from page 52)

Four hours later, I was finally comfortable that the situation was under control.

And my daughter wasn't even home yet. 🤣😂

But you can probably guess this isn't really an email about lice...

There's an important lesson in my lice madness.

Most people **would not have had the option** to go on a 4-hour lice escapade.

(We'll leave aside whether it was a good use of my time. 😜)

Most people are either working a J-O-B or have to live their lives according to their client's schedules.

Not me.

While I was learning more about lice that ANYONE ever needs to know... my business kept chugging right along without me.

That's the beauty of having an online business built around scalable products.

I'm not trading hours for dollars... and I'm very rarely working on urgent tasks.

So I can go on 4-hour lice-capades if I want to!

If you're struggling to find that kind of freedom in your business, the first step is to create a scalable product.

And for most entrepreneurs... that means creating an online course.

Online courses are generally the best way to serve more people without having to work more.

(continued on page 54)

(continued from page 53)

But let's get real for a second... creating an online course probably seems about as complicated as the whole "lice" thing did to me... Am I Right?

The good news is that it doesn't have to be.

And you don't have to scour the internets for an answer that may or may not be right!

Next week, my friend and mentor Amy Porterfield is hosting a brand new masterclass.

The 3 Behind-The-Scenes Secrets to Digital Course Success

Amy is THE digital course guru.

She's built her business — a business that's on pace to do eight figures this year — around digital courses.

She's launched 6 successful digital courses, and, in the training, Amy will spill the beans on how to build, launch, and grow a thriving digital course business without hiring a big team and without the overwhelm.

When you **sign up for the FREE training**, you'll learn:

- The major mindset shift that all successful digital course owners will need to adopt as they move forward.

- A simple recording strategy that dramatically cuts down on time and production costs, and still delivers an amazing course.

- The single MOST effective way to sell your online course, and why you need to know it from the outset.

And Amy will be sharing real life examples of digital courses that are raking in revenue and changing lives.

(continued on page 55)

(continued from page 54)

Reserve your spot at the Masterclass now.

You can thank me once you've built your business and have the freedom to go on a 4-hour lice-capade (or maybe doing something more useful with your day).

Talk later.

Bobby

P.S. This training is absolutely free, but if you choose to buy something from Amy, I'll get a commission (and you'll get some amazing bonuses from me too!).

Amy is **the only person** whose products I promote, and I actively recommended her products before I was an affiliate. So know that I recommend you **sign up for the masterclass no matter what**!

When I sent this email, I just thought the lice-capade was a funny story to explain to people the benefit of not having a business that tied me to my desk.[32] I never could have anticipated how many people would respond—not just to sign up, but to tell me about shampoos, tea tree oil, and other products and tricks to keep lice at bay.

Why did all those people feel the need to respond? It wasn't because I'd asked them to. As I said, I'd already fallen down some spectacular rabbit holes on lice eradication.

---

32. Note, my thinking about the best way to build an online business has changed quite a bit since 2019. I'm not opposed to trading hours for dollars (if it's *enough* dollars), and I most certainly don't think you're going to get rich by creating online courses. But that's a rant for another day (and maybe another book)!

Some of the people who responded were my serial respond-ers, the people who I had trained by engaging with them in the past. But most were not. All of them responded because they saw that I was having a problem, and they wanted to help me solve that problem.

And why did all these people want to help me?

Because they viewed me as a friend, and friends don't let friends get lice!

WRITE EMAILS LIKE YOU'RE WRITING TO A FRIEND

That lice-capade email led me to the number-one ~~secret~~[33] piece of advice I have for you about email: as much as possible, you should write marketing emails like you're writing to a friend.

If you look at the lice email (and pretty much all the emails reprinted in this book), you'll see that my email is written like I'm talking to a friend. And that's why the responses I got were exactly like the advice you'd get from friends. That doesn't happen if your emails seem like they come from a company. (I mean, it would be weird if Bed Bath & Beyond told you about its lice problem.)

But why is this important?

Think about your own email inbox. Pretty full, right?[34] When you open your inbox, what stands out among all those messages?

---

33. Speaking of friends, here's some friendly advice: run like hell from anyone claiming to have the "secret" to building a business. There are no secrets. The person claiming to have a secret either doesn't know that or is lying to you. Either way, you probably shouldn't be taking *that person's* advice!

34. I could make up a statistic, like "the average American gets 170 emails a day," but I'm too lazy to look it up and stats are boring. Plus, you thinking about your own inbox is going to be way more persuasive than any stat I could dig up.

Think about what you look at first. Probably not even the subject lines, right? If you're like me, you probably scan your new messages for emails from people you know and like. You look for the emails from friends, not ads and promos and messages from people selling to you. Even if those friends have businesses, and even if they ultimately have something to sell you, if they're writing emails that are interesting or fun to read or that otherwise bring value to your life, you're going to be excited to keep opening those emails.

On the other hand, I'm not going to be excited about reading yet another email from yet another person who is clearly just trying to sell me some stuff. At most, I might read the subject line, and if that person happens to be selling something I actually want right then, I might open it. Otherwise, it gets deleted, unsubscribed, even marked as spam. (This is why that selling concept of marketing that we talked about in Chapter 1 simply *does not* work.)

Bobby Breaks "Marketing"

Early on in my marketing days, I was told, "Don't make your weekly emails great. Save your great stuff for your sales emails." Luckily, I ignored that advice, 'cause it's bass-ackwards!

When you get a reputation for writing boring emails, guess what? Nobody opens your emails when it's time to sell. But can you guess what happens if you get a reputation for sending great emails? Hopefully, you said that people *do* open your emails, even when it comes time to sell.

> Every email we send is training our audience about what to
> expect from our emails. Best to train them to expect great things.

Because people are getting so many emails, our emails—just like everything else we do as marketers—have to help us stand out, to make us different, so people think, "I want to pay attention to Bobby. He has some stuff that is worth spending my time on."

When you become friends with your audience, when you help subscribers come to expect that your emails are worth their time investment, they don't care what the subject line is—they'll see your name and they'll want to open it. We'll talk more about the *how* in the coming chapters. For now, just understand that your goal is to turn your subscribers into friends.

Put yourself in your reader's shoes and ask how they decide what to spend their time on as a reader of emails. Then ask how *you* can position yourself to be in that coveted position where they open and read your emails, no matter what.

As with nearly everything in marketing, the 80/20 rule applies here. No matter how good you are at email, not everyone is going to like what you do (much less think of you as a friend). You should expect that 80 percent of the people on your list *won't* get to the point of really liking you, and that's okay.[35] Focus on the 20 percent of people who, when they see an email come from you, are going to open it regardless of anything else.

That 20 percent of your list? Those are your friends. When you've established yourself as a friend, and when you write your emails as

---

35. Not to brag, but I've turned the 80/20 rule on its head. Although opens aren't necessarily a mark of success, using the things I'm teaching you in this book, I've consistently had 80 percent of the people on my list engage with at least one email every thirty days.

coming from one friend (you) to another (the ride-or-die 20 percent of your list), your audience gets to know, like, and trust you. They're in for the entire journey. And that journey leads to raving fans, which gets more people into your world, which means…more friends!

YOU'VE GOT A FRIEND IN ME

Anytime you're writing an email, ask yourself, "Is this how I'd write to a friend? If I were writing it to a friend, is this how I would say it?" If the answer to either of these questions is no, *you're doing it wrong.*

Focusing on writing everything like you're writing to a friend ensures that the content, the structure, and the tone of your emails are right.

I guess I should include a caveat to this whole chapter: all of this is only true if you actually *like* your friends. If you're a bad friend, if you're one of those people who is mean to your friends, ignore this whole chapter and just do the opposite of whatever your instinct is.[36]

The other reason to write your emails like you're writing to a friend is to get rid of some of that pressure that comes with facing the dreaded blinking cursor: *What do I say and how do I say it so it'll sound good?*

I don't know about you, but when I write an email to a friend, I don't feel a lot of pressure to make it perfect. I don't feel like I have to get them to do anything. I just write something. And that's the first mindset shift you need to make: stop trying to be perfect, and just write an email to your friends!

---

36. Or maybe work on not being such a bad friend???

To be clear, writing emails like you're talking to a friend is not just about your tone or the words you use. A lot of people think that in order to make email fun, they should use flowery words or a lot of snark or sassy language. That may be fun copy, but just adding sass to a boring email isn't the point. If you write an email that sounds cool but is just rehashing your blog post, you're doing it wrong.

It's about approaching emails from a completely different angle. If you wanted to tell your friend about your weekly blog post or podcast, how would you do it? That's the question you should be asking.

Don't worry, we'll get to the how in a bit.

YOU'RE A FRIEND, NOT A KNOW-IT-ALL BLOWHARD

The advice in this chapter may sound counter to what some marketers preach, which is to set yourself up as *the* expert of your topic. After all, who can they trust more than the Ultimate Expert in Whatever You're Selling? You most definitely *should* set yourself up as the expert, but that doesn't mean you can't also position yourself as a friendly voice. It's the difference between being an approachable expert and a know-it-all blowhard.

Candidly, the issue of expertise isn't really relevant to most of the emails you'll be sending. In Part II, we'll talk about how to position yourself as a trusted expert at the outset. Once you've checked that box for your people, they really aren't looking for you to continually show them how smart you are. I don't know about you, but I don't particularly like being talked *at*, which is what happens when people try to use email to establish their authority. Let's avoid that, mmmkay?

If you get to the point where people are getting your regular weekly emails without having established a position of trust, you're screwed. I know that sucks to hear, but I want to be honest with you. People aren't going to stick around on your list if they haven't already concluded that you're someone who has some expertise that might be helpful to them. You should have established your authority *before* they joined your list (with a freebie) and right when they joined. (We'll go into this in Chapters 7 and 8 where I talk about the first few emails you send people.)

If you're paying attention, you might be thinking something like "Okay, I get why being a blowhard is bad, but what's so great about making people feel like I'm a friend?"

Wow, the you in my head asks great questions! Here's the answer: establishing yourself as a friend puts you in a truly unique position to influence people. I could do research and point to all kinds of studies and articles that would tell you that a referral from a friend is the most powerful marketing tool there is. I told my editor that my readers are perfectly competent to type something like "how important is word-of-mouth advertising" into Google. But she *insisted* that I do at least a little. Fine. How about this?

A Nielsen survey on trust and advertising returned some pretty telling numbers when asking what forms of advertising respondents trusted. Referral marketing scored the highest across every single demographic, out-doing editorial content, all forms of ads, and brand sponsorship.[37]

---

37. "15 Referral Marketing Statistics You Need To Know," *Extole*, https://www.extole.com/blog/15-referral-marketing-statistics-you-need-to-know/ (Visited May 14, 2021).

Did you catch that? Referral marketing is the *most trusted* form of marketing across all age ranges.

Although you aren't going to magically make the people in your audience forget that you're a marketer, if you work to position yourself as their friend, they'll start to trust your recommendations way more...even when you're recommending your own products! Put another way, considering that a recommendation from a friend is considerably *more powerful* than a recommendation from a standard marketer, you'd be crazy *not* to position yourself as a friend!

A quick note, though. As you're building this relationship with your list, don't forget that you are, first and foremost, a marketer. I am always very clear with my subscribers: "Look, I love you, but I'm running a business, so while you are very much my friends, I *am* going to sell to you." I don't try to hide that from people or pretend I'm not selling something, because it's not about being disingenuous. They know what the deal is, just like you do when you subscribe to someone's list.

And I'm not saying that by treating subscribers as friends, people are somehow going to forget that you're a marketer. You wouldn't want that. The goal is for them to know that you're their friend who has this business that serves people and who will send emails to them either way (because that's what friends do). But who, when it's right, may also be able to serve *them* through this business too.[38]

---

38. Note, like nearly every form of trust, the position of trusted friend is hard to get and easy to lose. In other words, be very careful about *what* you recommend to people. If your audience ever gets the feeling that you are recommending something just to make money, you're screwed.

WITH GREAT POWER COMES GREAT RESPONSIBILITY

Once you've made this mindset shift, you also have to recognize that the people on your list are going to think about the emails they get from you as coming from a friend—so be careful about how you use that power.

In March 2020, shortly after the first lockdown of the COVID-19 pandemic, I sent this email to my subscribers:

From: Bobby Klinck

Date: March 31, 2020

Subject: Please pray for Katie (my #2)…

Before you ask, no she isn't sick.

But she could *definitely* use your prayers today.

Now that she's been a full-time employee for three months (and on the job for five months), we are getting together for a whole day a planning.

Yeah, you read that right… she's going to be on a Zoom call with me ALL freaking day!

We'll be planning out a few affiliate promotions (including Ultimate Bundles, TRIBE, and Digital Course Academy) and putting together our internal plans for the year!

Can you imagine having to deal with my particular kind of crazy (and trying to control me) for a whole day!?!?

(continued on page 64)

(continued from page 63)

(On top of my normal level of wacky, by the time we start the meeting at 9 am her time -- noon my time -- I will be well into my second or third pot of coffee!)

So, like I said, she could definitely use your prayer today.

Those of you who've been following along for a while may be asking:

"Hold up Bobby... I thought you'd already planned your year?"

Well, we did plan the year, but things change.

The first quarter has taught us **a lot** about what we had planned... and this coronavirus thing has thrown wrenches into some of our plans.

So we are getting together to plan out the rest of the year.

That brings me to **today's episode of The Certified BADA$$ Online Marketing Podcast**, which is about the lessons I learned in the first quarter!

The lessons aren't unique to me... these are lessons that apply to YOU and your business (even if you don't know it yet).

And you can imagine there have been a few really big lessons with all the things shifting around us.

So after you've said a prayer for Katie... **go check out Episode 147 of The Certified BADA$$ Online Marketing Podcast**.

Talk later.

Bobby

P.S. If you aren't sure where you should be focused in your business right now, there's still time to grab your spot in the training put on by Mike Michalowicz: How to Find the ONE Big Thing You Should be Focused on in Your Business. Getting focused on the RIGHT things is a huge part of building a successful business, so grab your spot.

I said right up front that Katie wasn't sick. And I was just making fun of the fact that she was going to have to spend all day helping me, so I figured my readers would feel sorry for her.

The problem was, I hadn't thought about how my subscribers would read even just that subject line from the perspective of a friend. The people on my list feel like we have a relationship where I would tell them if someone on my team had COVID, and I would ask for their prayers, so they assumed that's what was happening with Katie—and although they were relieved to find out that wasn't the case, they were pissed that I made them think for even a second that she might be sick because of the subject line.

I'm guessing that if my emails were boring, like most, my audience wouldn't have had this reaction. Of course, boring emails would never have used that subject line either. At any rate, becoming a trusted friend is a double-edged sword, so be careful how you use it.

How are you feeling? Still along for the ride? That's awesome, because we're going to learn something *so* important in the next chapter: why we need to start by killing all the lawyers![39]

---

39. Lawyer Bobby has insisted that I include a very clear disclaimer. Please don't *literally* kill all the lawyers. Actually, don't *literally* kill any of the lawyers (or anyone else!). Okay, on with the show!

CHAPTER 4

THE FIRST THING WE DO, LET'S KILL ALL THE LAWYERS

ON JANUARY 29, 2019, I sent an email with the subject line "What do Russian strippers, Australia, and content marketing have in common?"

Can you guess the answer? Well, here, why don't I just let you read it for yourself?

From: Bobby Klinck

Date: January 29, 2019

Subject: What do Russian Strippers, Australia, and Content Marketing have in common?

That's a pretty good subject line, huh?

(continued on page 68)

(continued from page 67)

(Gotta love a marketer who gives him self a pat on the back right up front! 😄)

I'm gonna give you a minute to think about the answer to that riddle… and tell you about my friend who first inspired me to write subject lines like that one.

Her name is Jillian Bowen.[40]

I met Jillian through an online group run by Amy Porterfield. We interacted a few times online and were even on a group Zoom chat at one point.

But Jillian truly became my friend when we met in real life at an event in August.

She's one of those people who has a knack for sizing someone up in about 2 seconds… and she immediately knew I needed someone who'd take me down a notch (or 7).

During the two day event, she pretty much kept me in stitches the whole time. She always seemed to have the perfect thing to say to take a subtle dig at me in an amusing way.

(Don't worry… she was much nicer to most of the other people there!)

But I'm not telling you about her because she made fun of me… she's also helped me get out of "Lawyer Man" mode and into "Fun Bobby" mode.

She's the one who gave me the guts to use my most memorable subject line to date ("Why are you sending me pictures of you with random women?").

(continued on page 69)

---

40. In case you're wondering, yes…*that* Jillian.

(continued from page 68)

But back to the riddle...

...have you figured out the answer yet?

This might help... Jillian is a content strategist who lives in Australia.

And she's my guest on this week's episode of The Online Genius Podcast.

I'm not going near the Russian Stripper thing with a ten foot pole... you'll have to give the episode a listen to hear her tell that story.

The great thing is that Jillian is kind of like me... she loves to teach online entrepreneurs how to do things, and her forte is content (and social media).

In the episode, she pretty much gives a masterclass (and no, I'm not talking about the sales kind) on content strategy. She delivers SO much value.

If you want to get your content marketing strategy in order, this is THE episode to check out.

So go give the episode a listen.

And if nothing else, you may hear Jillian take me down a notch or two...

Talk later.

Bobby

P.S. Jillian taught me pretty much everything useful I know about content marketing, so if you appreciate what I'm doing... you really should pay attention to Jillian. And a good place to start is with this week's episode. Stop reading... go listen.

At the same time I was writing this email, I was writing a mediation brief for a legal case involving something like $10 million. As I was going back and forth between writing both of these, I thought to myself, "I better make sure I don't confuse these two documents and put a reference to Russian strippers in the mediation brief." That probably wouldn't have ended well (though it would have livened things up!).

But here's the thing: there's *no way* you would ever mix up those two documents. The mediation brief was written with perfect grammar, using a formal tone and lots of boring footnotes. That brief sounds nothing like me.

And the email…well, the email sounds *exactly like me*. Which is exactly how it's supposed to sound. When I'm writing emails, I take the Bard's advice from Henry VI, and the first thing I do is kill all the lawyers (or at least the lawyer personality)!

WHAT A BAD HANGOVER TAUGHT ME ABOUT EMAIL

No, not *that* kind of hangover! I'm talking about the movie trilogy. And specifically, the worst of the three…

In *The Hangover Part II*, Stu is set to get married, and his father-in-law-to-be's speech at the rehearsal dinner is really the only truly great part of the movie. The father-in-law explained that he didn't like Stu at first but then realized he is like *khao*, soft white rice in lukewarm water. A bland, tasteless dish that would never offend anyone but is utterly forgettable.

Too many people write emails that are *khao*, bland and utterly forgettable.

That might be fine for a mediation brief, but not for a weekly email. As we've already discussed, my weekly email to my subscribers is supposed to build connections with an audience of friends, as part of the journey we are on together. The only way that email can do its job is if I let people get to know me, quirks and all. I'm building the know, like, and trust factor with *my people* by letting them get to know *the real me.*

Do my emails offend some people? Yep.

Do I care? Nope.

There's a concept out there: love me or hate me; there's no money in between. In other words, people who strive to be bland to cater to everyone end up speaking to no one because no one hears it—it's too boring.

Let me be clear; you only have two choices here:

1. You can be boring, so nobody pays attention to you.

2. Or you can be you—which means you *will* turn some people off.

The people who don't resonate with the real you will leave, but the people who do resonate with you will be well on their way to being your raving fans. And that's what you're going for: to get the people who are meant to be your followers to really listen, to stick around, and to become your ultimate true fans.

You can't attract the right people if you're not willing to repel the wrong people.

Do you really want to attract an audience of people who are going to be offended by the real you? Do you want to live every moment of every day self-conscious about who you are? That sounds like living hell to me. Or, even worse, do you want to change who you are to fit the idea of who these people—people who aren't even your true fans—think you should be?

The last thing you want to do is show up one way publicly and then act differently after people buy and actually start interacting with you. (Kinda like if you market a movie as a romantic comedy...the two leading characters damn well better end up together in the end.)[41] When they meet the real you and don't like that person because it's not who they thought they were buying from, they're probably gonna be pissed!

Instead of pretending to be something you're not, you should show people who you truly are and let them get to know the real you from the beginning. You are building a business around people you like, people you think of as friends that you want to spend time helping. And this is a long-term relationship you're getting into.

We are all naturally attracted to people who are somewhat like us. I have collected an audience of people who are snarky yet giving because that's what I am.[42] The people who find me and stick around do so because they're like me and they think, "I want to hang out with him, have a beer with him, and maybe learn a thing or two from him."

Political pundits and pollsters actually ask people which candidate they'd rather have a beer with because they know the answer to that question holds a lot of value. People are way more likely to vote for the person they think of as more likable and relatable, and the same is true in business. If you have your choice to buy from someone you don't know much about and who is just kind of blah versus someone like you, who you get along with, and who you'd like to have a beer with...it's a pretty easy choice.

---

41. I'm looking at you here, Kevin Smith, cause that shit you pulled with *Chasing Amy* is not cool in my book.

42. And you're still reading this, so that's likely who you are too! Hello, friend!

But here's the real insight: we're not all going to want to have a beer with the same type of person. If we all liked the same people, that bar would get really crowded. (And, hey, maybe you don't want to have a beer at all. Maybe you judge people by who you'd like to get a martini with, or coffee, or a soy-vanilla green juice. Doesn't matter—what matters is finding the people you'd like to hang out with casually because those are the people you're ultimately going to want to do business with.)

Celebrate Unsubscribes

Most people get all freaked out when people unsubscribe from their list (and you'll see people asking what a "normal" unsubscribe rate is). Not me. I celebrate unsubscribes.

When someone unsubscribes from your list, you might think, "Oh my god, they hate me! I'm a horrible person." Quit being so overdramatic because it means no such thing. It means one of two things: either they don't really need your service, or you're just not their cup of tea. And that's 100 percent okay. I am clearly not for *a lot* of people. A lot.[43]

The only way you're going to have no one unsubscribe from your list is if you don't email at all or if you are totally vanilla. That sure as hell isn't going to turn anyone into a raving fan (or do much of anything to serve your business).

---

43. For some reason that I don't quite understand, my editor and team insisted that I stress that *a lot* of people are annoyed by me. Not sure why...

> Your goal isn't to have a boring conversation with everyone. Your goal should be to have the perfect conversation with the right people. Know that getting people to unsubscribe means you're doing it right. You're building the relationships that connect with your people, the people who want to be there because they know, like, and trust you—so they're going to stick around.

CURSE LIKE A SAILOR

I always want to sound like myself, so my emails should sound like me talking. Ideally, you want the subscribers who have heard you talk—in person, on your podcast, in interviews or videos—to hear *your actual voice* when they read your emails.

That means that if you curse like a sailor in real life, then curse like a sailor in your emails.

I'm not afraid to curse in my emails sometimes because I curse sometimes when I talk. I don't do it all the time or for the shock value; it's just how I talk. And I warn people that it's coming early on—in the very beginning of my welcome sequence (which we'll look at more in Chapter 8)—"Buckle up…it's gonna get weird!"

And this doesn't just apply to *how* you talk. It also extends to what you talk about and the references you make. If you're geeky, let it out! I make *Seinfeld* references in my emails and in real life all the time. It drives me nuts because no one in my real life enjoys *Seinfeld* as much as I do, so they all make fun of me. Other people refer to *Star Wars* or *Star Trek* or comic books because those things are what they relate to—and the people in their audiences love those references!

Remember that you are writing emails to your friends. If you would make that *Star Wars* reference or *Seinfeld* joke with your friends, why not throw it into your email?

Similarly, if you care deeply about politics and you want to talk about it, why not talk about it? Yes, you're ~~probably~~[44] going to piss off people on the other side, but people on your side will be with you.

You might be thinking I'm just telling you to be polarizing cause you've heard that's what you're supposed to do. When I was speaking at an event, someone actually asked, "How do you go about being so polarizing?" I had to laugh. I don't have to *try* to be polarizing; being me does the trick just fine.

The good news is that the same is true for you. ~~Just be yourself.~~ Don't try to be polarizing or come up with shocking things to say simply for the shock value. Be polarizing on things you truly believe in, and do it by being yourself, not by being intentionally abrasive or hurting people's feelings.

We're not doing this to shock people; we're doing it to connect with them.

DON'T WRITE LIKE THE QUEEN OF ENGLAND (UNLESS YOU *ARE* THE QUEEN OF ENGLAND—HEY, LIZZIE!)

I have yet to meet someone who speaks in proper King's English. Nearly everyone I've ever met uses colloquialisms, ends sentences in prepositions, speaks in sentence fragments, splits infinitives,

---

44. I feel confident that there is no need to hedge on this statement!

and dangles participles.[45] Yet they seem to think their grammar has to be perfect when they write emails.

When I was a prosecutor working with police officers and federal agents, I would have to work hard to prepare them before they testified—not about what they were going to say, but about how they would say it.

They wanted to say, "The female exited the vehicle."

"No," I would say. "The woman got out of the car."

I wanted to just yell, "Speak like a human, not a robot!"

But it wasn't their fault. That's how they were trained to write their reports, even though that's not how they would have said it if they were talking to ~~their friends~~ anyone. So I spent almost my entire prep time with them getting them to speak like human beings again.

We're the same way—we've been trained to use proper grammar and follow the rules of English when we write. But because very few people actually speak that way, when we speak conversationally and write formally, it comes off as very stiff and stilted.

So split those infinitives and dangle all the participles you want.[46]

HERE'S *HOW* TO WRITE LIKE YOU TALK

By now, I'm guessing you're convinced that you should write like you talk. But you're probably wondering what that actually

---

45. Okay, I actually don't really know what a dangling participle is, but my editor assures me we all use them. Ignoring her edits, dangling participles have popped up throughout this book. That's right, grammar nerds…I just dropped an inside joke just for you!

46. Here's hoping my English teachers aren't reading this book. If you are, Ms. Callahan… sorry, but not really.

looks like. Luckily, you "know a guy" who has a solution. Try the following exercise:

- Set up a few calls with friends, on Zoom or any other platform that lets you record the call.

- Talk with your friends about whatever you want, however you would normally talk. No agenda, just a chat.

- Record the calls, but try not to talk differently or pay attention to the recording while you're chatting with your friends.

- Have the recording transcribed, and look at the cadence of how you actually talk when you're talking to a friend.

- Try to adopt that in your writing.

If you talk like Hemingway, write like Hemingway. Use short sentences. If you talk like James Joyce…there's something very wrong with you. Knock it off.[47]

This exercise helps you find your own *voice*, which is basically the choice of words you use and how you put your words together. Do you speak in long run-on sentences or shorter, choppy sentences? I go off on tangents all the time. (Here's guessing that anyone still reading has figured that one out already!)

Tone, on the other hand, is about how your mind works, which is reflected in how you speak. I could use the same words

---

47. I'm kidding, obviously. If you really, truly talk how James Joyce writes, then I guess you should write your emails just like that. (Forgive me in advance for never subscribing.)

as someone else, but my tone would likely come across as snarkier or jokier. What tone do you want for *your* brand?

Tone has to do with the emotion that comes through in your writing, the way it makes people feel. Again, I tend to be snarky, which makes people feel amused. Other people may be tenderhearted, which makes people feel inspired or warm and fuzzy. Another person might be very serious.

The tone you want your business to have should align with your voice, but it's not about word choice. It's about the emotion, the feel of it. It can be hard to define, but ultimately it's about what is evoked when people read your emails or interact with your business—the emotional triggers you're trying to press.

And this can change over time, especially if you've been very vanilla without having much of a tone or voice at all up to this point. If that's you—if you've been inoffensively bland—let your tone out. Your audience is waiting to hear the *real* you!

HOPPY EASTER

My most famous email ever went out Easter week, with the subject line "I really don't like Sweet Baby Jesus."

Yup.

Now, before *you* become one of the people who either has an extreme response or who hits unsubscribe…just read the email:

From: Bobby Klinck

Date: April 16, 2019

Subject: I really don't like Sweet Baby Jesus…

Before you get pissed… I'm not being sacrilegious on Easter week.

I'm talking about a beer.

To be more specific, I'm talking about a chocolate, peanut butter atrocity called "Sweet Baby Jesus!"

Just writing this email is making me queasy!

The beauty of beer is in its simplicity.

You can make amazingly complicated flavors from just 4 ingredients: water, malted barley, hops, and yeast.

The quickest way to ruin beer is by trying to get fancy (e.g., adding peanut butter and chocolate to it)!

So why am I telling you this about beer?

Because we do the same freaking thing with our businesses!

We sometimes ruin things by adding the metaphorical peanut butter and chocolate when we really don't need to.

Business is kinda like beer… its beauty is in its simplicity.

What if I told you that you could "keep it simple stupid" and still have great results?

Well, you can.

(continued on page 80)

(continued from page 79)

In this week's episode of The Online Genius Podcast, I break down the results of my recent "non-launch" launch of The Online Genius Template Library.

I can't claim to have had a stroke of genius to keep it simple... getting busy in my law firm business forced me hand.

But then a funny thing happened.

When I stripped it down and kept it simple, I ended up with my most profitable promotion yet!

A few emails over a 3-day period generated $58k in revenue.

And because there were no ads or other costs, it was 100% profit.

I don't know about you, but a simple, stress-free promotion that generates more revenue than ever is my kinda simple!

If you'd like to hear more about how I did it, head over and check out Episode 74 of The Online Genius Podcast.

Talk later.

Bobby

The very first response I got when I sent out this email was from a friend who is a copywriter and who happens to run a faith-based business. She wrote, "I was about to be mad at you, but that's about the best use of a shocking subject line I've ever gotten. You defused it perfectly in the next line."

My people get me. They get that I might say something truly ridiculous, but they know where my heart is. And I probably did lose some people, sure. (Let's be honest, you can never weed everybody out in advance.) My team and I work to actively weed people out so my list is made up of people who truly want to be there—as shown by at least a third of them opening every email.

Okay, are you with me so far? Write emails like you're writing to a friend. Write emails in your voice. But what the hell should you write those emails *about*?

Well, let me tell you a story.

Ha, made you look, didn't I? You'll have to turn to Chapter 5 to get that.

CHAPTER 5

"WOOHOO, A NEWSLETTER," SAID NO ONE, EVER

REMEMBER THAT FIRST *GOOD* EMAIL I SENT, the one I showed you in the Introduction? Well, this is the email I sent after that one:

From: Bobby Klinck

Date: September 4, 2018

Subject: Screw more cowbell… we need more Liberty Bell!!!

Hey Jillian,

Wouldn't it be great to get to hang out with 400+ like-minded online entrepreneurs and get insight from Amy Porterfield, Marie Forleo, Jasmine Star, and Tarzan Kay?!?

(continued on page 84)

(continued from page 83)

Well, I got the privilege to do just that, and in this week's podcast episode I lay out the 5 key takeaways from an amazing weekend.

But first, I want to tell you about this woman who will say ANYTHING…

The event was part of a "bonus" package I got from signing up to Marie Forleo's B-School through Amy Porterfield's affiliate link.

As part of the bonus package, I also got the pleasure of interacting with the other B-Schoolers in a private Facebook group.

The week before, I put together a quick "explainer" video for my law firm website remodel that is in the works and posted it for comments in the group.

The general consensus was that the messaging was really good, but that it needed something…

Then came this awesome woman named Mel who posted a GIF from Saturday Night Live with the simple comment:

Needs more cowbell!

For those of you who haven't seen the skit, it's a classic in which Christopher Walken is playing a music producer who is insisting that Will Farrell's character needs to add more cowbell to a song.

But I digress… back to the story.

Mel explained that what was missing was ME. She explained that the reason she and the other members of the group wanted to do business with my company was because of me.

I have to admit… that is something that I have struggled with for a LONG time. I've always felt like my product should be front and center, and I kinda thought this Bobby guy should be in the background.

(continued on page 85)

(continued from page 84)

Mel assured me I was wrong.

But then again, she's someone who is REALLY comfortable being herself. Heck, here's a picture she posted to the group of her being silly in the airport:

If it were just Mel giving me this advice, it would be easy enough to dismiss it... I mean she really is someone who is comfortable saying anything to anybody!

But talking with the other entrepreneurs at the conference convinced me...

The other entrepreneurs I was with at the conference expressed to me that they loved ME first and foremost. They could get legal information other places... what they responded to and connected with was me.

And they assured me that they wanted even more of me in the brand. To quote Mel, they all wanted "more cowbell."

That brings me back to this week's podcast episode...

In this week's episode of The Online Genius Podcast, I walk through the five biggest takeaways I got from the weekend with these amazing online entrepreneurs.

(continued on page 86)

(continued from page 85)

As you can probably imagine from this email, one of the lessons was about adding more cowbell. In the episode, I talk a bit more about this realization and explain how that is going to mean some changes around here.

You'll also hear me explain:

- The value of creating a personal connection.

- Why your team is crucial to the success of your business.

- The importance of getting out of your comfort zone.

- Why you need to find your people.

- The importance of a mentor who is authentic.

It's a REALLY good episode if I do say so myself...

Click here to check out my pearls of wisdom in this week's episode.

I look forward to sharing more of me, my journey, and my struggles with you in future episodes (along with interviews of some dynamite guests!). So you are really going to want to continue to tune into the show.

Talk later.

Bobby

P.S. As an epilogue to the story, after Mel got home from the conference, she posted a video of her and her daughter ringing a huge "Liberty Bell." She said that after meeting me, she was convinced that a cowbell wasn't big enough... she wanted me to bring more Liberty Bell to my brand. So I've printed a sign that sits in front of my computer that says: "Screw more cowbell... we need more Liberty Bell!!!" It serves as my constant reminder to put myself at the forefront of my business.

After I sent this email, I got a response from a woman who said, "I've been on your list for a long time, and this is the first time I've felt like you're a real person, not a company…and it's the first time I've wanted to do business with you."

For those of you keeping track at home: yes, this means that I sent out emails that got good responses *twice in a row*! And I'm like Pavlov's dogs—I'm easily trainable. When Bobby gets good responses…he does more of whatever got him that reward.[48]

LET ME TELL YOU A STORY

Up to this point, this book has been kind of abstract. I mean, "Write like you're writing to a friend" isn't exactly step-by-step how-to advice. You may have been screaming something like "Get to the freaking point already!" at the book. Good news… it's all been building to this final chapter of Part I, where I share the single trick to help you actually put theory into practice.

Are you ready?

Instead of writing *about content*, you should *tell stories*.[49]

But what do I mean by that? Most people send emails that summarize the weekly content they are creating on their podcast, blog, YouTube channel, or whatever other medium they're using. And they probably do this because they've been told they need to send an email each week and desperately don't want to have to create anything other than the content that's already created. Sorry to tell you, that easy button's not gonna work out well for you.

---

48. Yes, I just referred to myself in the third person. Get over it. Especially you, Jillian!

49. What, you were expecting some super-secret ninja trick? Nope. Stories. That's it.

Some people try to add some sizzle to their content steak by hiring copywriters to punch up their emails to make them sound fun—and they pay a pretty penny to do it. But the emails are just punched up regurgitation of their content. The emails could have come from anybody because there's nothing about *them* in it.

Not throwing stones here, 'cause *I used to do this too.* My emails used to just summarize what was in my podcast, which, as we now know, is the dumbest thing ever! People don't even click on a link in an email to go listen to podcasts. They listen to them all in one place, like Spotify, Google, or Apple Podcasts, where they can see if you put out a new episode.

An email that rehashes content will be irrelevant to basically everyone. If they are interested in your podcasts or videos, they can just skip the email and consume the content. And if they're *not* interested, there's no reason for them to read your email either. (Sidenote: an email that summarizes content is basically transactional. You're trying to "sell" your content to get the click.)

While content-driven emails suck, story-based emails are the bomb dot-com. When your goal is just to brighten their day with a story, every email you send can be valuable to every person on your list. When they are getting that kind of value, they will continue to read your emails even if they don't need what you have right now.

As an added bonus, when you shift to story-based emails, they get way easier to write. When you write a story, there's no pressure to figure out how to write it perfectly or how to get the click. Instead, you can just relax and talk about yourself a bit (and we all love to do that).

Added bonus number two: telling stories is actually a better way to teach your audience. Humans are wired to learn through stories. Parables, allegories, and fables are so powerful because they teach lessons through story. If I asked if you were the tortoise or the hare, you would immediately think "slow and steady wins the race." Stories are a powerful way to share a core idea.

Before you say, "But, Bobby, you still tell people about your content." Well, duh! I'm not saying you shouldn't mention your podcast or posts. I'm saying that your content should not be the main focus of the email; *the story should be*. People don't open my email to find out about my podcast. They open it for the story and to connect with me. And whether that content is relevant to them that week or not, they still have a reason to connect.

The concept of writing story-based emails flows through every email you send—weekly emails, promo emails, and more, which you'll see in Part II. So you should start thinking in terms of story *now*, because that's what builds connection and makes your audience want to keep reading.

ANATOMY OF A STORY-BASED EMAIL

Since you haven't thrown this book into the trash (at least, not yet), I'm guessing you're at least open to the idea that I *might* be right[50] and would love for me to get to the how already.

There is a three-part structure to use for writing story-based emails:

---

50. Wow, those hedge words ("guessing," "open," "might") are making my editor's brain explode about now.

1. The Hook

2. The Story

3. The Call to Action

Each part will link to the next, so they are all part of a single journey. Let's take a look at each part in turn.

Part One: The Hook

The hook is just a fancy copywriting term for something that is going to get people interested—something to catch your audience's attention. Generally, this is going to be the subject line.

It could be the moment of high drama in the story, like I used with "Why are you sending me pictures of you with random women?!" These types of hooks are often—but not always—quotes from the story. Another example is the subject line I used to describe the moment I left my prior law firm unexpectedly: "How I found myself holding a three-month-old baby with no job."[51]

It can be curiosity-driven, where it makes someone reading it say, "Wait...what?" This might be something like "How did THAT get me in trouble?"[52] Another example from one of my most engaged emails of all time was simply "They're okay..." The

---

51. Yes, grammar police officer, I know that sentence is structured wrong. The "with no job" clearly should *not* be modifying "baby."

52. When someone reads that headline, something inside them just *has* to know what "*that*" is referring to.

reader can't help but wonder who the "they" is in that line and why they wouldn't be okay.

The hook could be a shock headline, like I used with the whole "I really don't like Sweet Baby Jesus." Use these sparingly and, when you do, defuse them immediately in the first line or two of the email.

Your hook can really be anything that will make people open, but generally speaking, you should use one of these three techniques to write your hook and get people interested in reading on.

Part Two: The Story

The story is a personal vignette from your life that ties into the theme of your email. It's an episode from your world that will help drive home the main idea or theme you are trying to get across in your email (generally the lesson from your call to action; see below).

Although there's no hard-and-fast rule about how long the story should be, generally you should be thinking *Seinfeld* not *Game of Thrones*. In other words, the best stories are generally the brief moments and encounters in your life that you can use to tell a story. Beyond the stories you've already seen about things like lice, Sweet Baby Jesus, being photobombed, a speech I made in high school, and others, here are some of the story topics I've used for my emails:

- A friend's dad telling us to *never* pass up a chance to use the restroom

- Me seeing people doing the walk of shame but not realizing that's what was happening

- Harvard Law School profs teaching us with movies like *My Cousin Vinny*

- Getting the song "Barbie Girl" stuck in my head

The point is that they are little moments in life that you can use to make a point. Because your main goal is to connect with your people, the story is the *main course* of your email. The story is what will make the email valuable for you and for your audience, so it will generally be the longest part of the email, and you should spend the majority of your effort writing the story.

Part Three: The Call to Action

The call to action is where you'll get the main theme or idea for the email. It involves you asking your readers to do something (even though we aren't fixated on whether they click). If you are creating long-form content (e.g., blog posts, podcasts, videos), the call to action asks people to click through to check out the content. It will generally include you asking a couple of times for people to click a link with a few quick paragraphs in between. Those paragraphs should not summarize the content; they are about creating curiosity around the content.

If you aren't creating long-form content, I have to misquote Jim Lovell and say, "Houston, we have a problem."[53] If you want to build a business based on your knowledge and expertise,

---

53. I say misquote because he actually said it in the past tense: "Houston, we've had a problem." That quote is considerably less quotable, which is probably why it is almost always misquoted.

creating regular content is really a must (but that's a subject for another book). If you aren't *yet* creating long-form content, then your call to action in the email should be some sort of a tip or idea that you want to share. Then you will ask your people to take action tied to that tip or lesson.

WRITE IT BACKWARDS

The ~~secret~~ trick to writing these emails is that you write them *backwards*, starting with the call to action first. Or, at least, you should create the plan for these emails backwards. You know, because of the whole "begin with the end in mind" thing.[54] You can't write anything in your email until you know what the call to action will be because how in the world can you write an email if you don't know where you plan to go with it in the end?

You don't have to write the call to action first, but you do need to know the *message* from the call to action before you can write the story because the story needs to be one that ties into that central message. And you have to write the story before you can find the right hook because the hook is related to the story.

Let's walk through the process of writing an email using my lice email from Chapter 3 as the example. The call to action in that email was to sign up for a launch about creating an online course, and the core message I wanted to draw out was that you

---

54. Stephen R. Covey, *The 7 Habits of Highly Effective People*, 25th anniv. ed. (New York: Simon & Schuster, 2013), 102. (But, really…did we need a footnote for this one?!?!?)

are limited when you're in a place where you are always trading hours for dollars. The related point is that you have freedom when you get out of the constant grind of one-to-one service. That was the *message* I wanted to convey.

From there, the goal was to find a story from my life that would drive home the "freedom" message. Immediately, I knew that finding an example of me frittering away time during the week would work. The lice-capade was a perfect story because it had literally just happened, and I'd spent several hours going down to the depths of the internets to research lice remedies. Because the email was being sent in September, my audience would know that this was something happening basically in real time, which was an added bonus.

A Note About Stories

When picking a story, ideally you don't want it to be too on point. The more that a reader has to wonder, "What the hell does this story have to do with (whatever it is you do)?" the better. In my case, I know people are saying, "How in the world is Bobby going to land this plane and bring it back to building a business or marketing? *What is going through his mind?*" Stories that are not *directly* on point tend to work better because they let you draw an analogy that will be more relatable to your audience. Part of what you're trying to do is to help people see things in a new way. Ideally your stories should be an analogy of sorts rather than a direct example of you teaching a lesson.

If you use a story that's directly related to the subject, you won't help convince anyone who wasn't already on board. For example, if someone reading my email is already convinced of my view on marketing, then they don't really need the lesson. But you're talking to people who haven't yet gotten it, so telling the story can provide a different angle for them to relate to and say, "Oh, I get it now!"

A concrete example may help. I was recently doing a guest training in a friend's program, and one of her students wanted to get across the message that women need to stop looking for men who are gorgeous because that doesn't lead to good things.[55] Her initial idea was to tell stories of when she had made that same mistake in dating and things did not end well. But I challenged her to come up with *other* stories that might convince people that you shouldn't judge a book by its cover. Any example where she bought something because it looked nice but turned out to be a piece of junk would do! By using other examples, she'd be more likely to convince her followers.

From there, it was just a matter of picking out the hook. In this case, I figured the reference to lice would be pretty compelling in itself and landed on "My 4-hour lice-capade..." as a curiosity hook, figuring people would just *have* to know what lice-related task had taken four hours of my life.

You've seen several of my emails throughout this book (with more to come in Part II), so you can look at those for examples of hooks, stories, and calls to action.

---

55. I express no opinion on the merits of this message...I'm just telling you the story! But if she's right, I guess it's a good thing that I only have a radio voice and not movie-star good looks.

CURIOSITY GOOD...TRICKS BAD!

When we were talking about the hook above, I said that curiosity hooks are one way to go. You open a loop that people have to close by reading the email. While using curiosity *is* good... tricks are bad.

Yet some people are literally telling you to trick your audience. Case in point: I was watching a training from one of the major digital marketing training companies and the teacher was trying to bolster his credibility by bragging that he "knows *all the tricks* to get people to open emails!" He meant that as a reason to listen to him...but for me it was a reason to say, "I'm out." Someone bragging about tricking people is about the best reason *not* to listen to them, in my book.[56]

Why are tricks bad? Well, you should be using email to build the know, like, and *trust* factor, to connect with your audience and to build virtual friendships with them. If you're using tricks to get people to open, is that doing any of those things? Of course not. Using tricks and gimmicks destroys trust and will result in people leaving in droves.

Instead of relying on tricks, the plan should be for people to open (and stick around) because your emails are so good.

There is a particular type of trick that is worth shaming specifically, and that is any trick that is about deception. Apparently, some email marketing teachers tell people to sometimes add "Re:" or "Fwd:" to the beginning of their subject line to make it look like they are responding to you or forwarding an email. Others are apparently teaching people to use subject lines like

---

56. Which is what you're reading, so there.

"In regards to our call" or "Our call later today" so it seems they are talking about a call you have directly with the person (when the "call" is actually a webinar).

If my grandmother were still around, she'd surely ask that whoever is teaching these approaches go "pick their switch."[57] Those subject lines are lies, plain and simple. And apparently this needs saying: lying is bad.

When you get a reputation for writing good emails, people will open them regardless of the subject line. So if you're doing the other things you're learning in this book, your subject line isn't going to matter that much.

GIVE 'EM A WIN

Everything you do should be intended to give some kind of "win" or value to your audience. If you're writing the standard regurgitated-content emails, you are not giving them value. In fact, you might just be stealing their sunshine.[58] But when you tell a meaningful story, you give people a win, no matter what.

Aside from the valuable insights in my emails, I give people a smile or a chuckle (mostly at my own expense). That is something the world can use more of. Other people provide inspiration or hope—and the world can use more of that too. When you have the approach of thinking, "Hey, someone can read this in five minutes or less and they will get something out of it; it will

---

57. If you aren't familiar with the expression, my grandmother would have us pick the limb she would use to give us a whipping when we were bad.

58. If you now have the Len song in your head…you are welcome!

bring some value to their day," it changes the way you look at your email marketing.

Some people say, "But, Bobby, I'm not funny." My wife and daughter would certainly tell you that I'm not funny, so we're in good company!

The reality is that I'm no comedian; I just tell stories. Sometimes they end up being funny, but they're not all funny. You most certainly don't have to go for the laugh. A great email is one that causes *any* emotional response. It can be happiness, a chuckle, inspiration, motivation, or anything that brightens your audience's day. If it will put an expression on their face, even momentarily, you've done your job because the emotion is where you connect.

And the emotion doesn't always have to be a positive one. You don't have to choose funny or snarky as your default approach. That's what I've chosen because I'm basically Chandler from *Friends*—I go for the laugh even when I'm uncomfortable. Your goal isn't to be Bobby,[59] your goal is to be you.

JUST JOKING!

A little earlier in the chapter, I told you that tricks are bad because you shouldn't lie to your friends (and I stand by that).

That doesn't mean that you can't mess with your friends, though.

---

59. This just in: my editor, my team, my family, and everyone who knows me implores you *not* to be like me. Apparently, one Bobby is more than enough.

Sometimes I like to play little pranks on people.[60] These pranks are different from tricks because they're not mean-spirited. They're more like inside jokes because we're all friends.

Here's an example:

From: Bobby Klinck

Sent: January 7, 2020

Subject: Where were you on May 14, 1998?

I was sitting on my couch in Austin, Texas, glued to the TV.

How about you?

Wait, you're telling me you don't remember that day specifically…

Come on, Jillian, that was the day of the Seinfeld finale.

The show that gave us phrases like "close-talker," "anti-dentite," and "yada, yada, yada."

And gave us characters like the Bubble Boy, the Soup Nazi and his famous "no soup for you," and Newman!

Seinfeld wasn't a TV show. It was a cultural phenomenon.

Even people who never watched the show use phrases from the show because they've become staples of our culture.

(continued on page 100)

---

60. My team would like to strenuously object to the use of the word "sometimes" in this sentence. Apparently, I prank people almost all the time.

(continued from page 99)

All that from a show about nothing.

The finale was a seminal moment in its own right. Even people who didn't watch the show regularly knew about it… and many shared the experience.

Because when something as important as Seinfeld wraps up, you want to be part of the experience.

Well, my friend… today is another one of those days where you are going to want to make sure you're part of the experience.

Because today I released the last episode of The Online Genius Podcast ever.

WTF?!?!?! 😳 🔫 😫

Yeah, as I was putting together my plan for 2020, The Online Genius Podcast just didn't have a place anymore.

But unlike the Seinfeld finale… this episode doesn't suck. It's actually a doozy that you won't want to miss.

If this episode were a man, it would be "sponge-worthy."

In it, I share my plans for 2020, which are pretty stinking epic.

And you know you want to hear what's next for this unorthodox Harvard Lawyer turned online entrepreneur who sends you emails about Seinfeld.

So do yourself a favor…go check out the last episode ever of The Online Genius Podcast

Talk later.

Bobby

Now, reading that email, you're probably pretty sad that the podcast is ending, right? I got so many people begging me not to take it away. Someone even replied to say, "I hope this is clickbait!"[61]

The secret that I revealed on the podcast itself was that we were re-branding, so the *Online Genius Podcast* was becoming *The Certified BADA$$ Online Marketing Podcast*. I was messing with my readers, but with a good payoff at the end.

Although not in email, I did this again when I teased my new BADA$$ Online Marketing University and got everybody super hyped up and asking where they could sign up, literally putting their credit card numbers in the chat. Then I revealed that it would be completely free.

These kinds of pranks are the kinds you might play on friends, pranks that ultimately over-deliver and make people excited after the reveal. That playfulness is part of my reputation. Apparently, I'm "rascally." I'm known for making what seem like cryptic statements and then revealing a little more and then a little more. It's fun!

When done right, playing pranks is just another part of creating an emotional response in people—even if that response is "That Bobby, he got me again!" As long as they're laughing while they say it, I'll take it!

And now it's time for me to tell you something that's no joke: you've reached the end of Part I!

Part I was all about the mindset shift to make before writing emails so that every subscriber becomes a friend. Now it's time to move into Part II, which will tell you more about how to connect with your new friends so that when you are ready to sell…they are eager to buy.

---

61. It's like they know me or something.

PART II

THE JOURNEY TO DOING EMAIL RIGHT

BELIEVE IT OR NOT, the summer *after* you graduate from law school can be way harder than law school itself. Before you're allowed to actually practice law, you have to take a three-day bar exam that is a mix of multiple-choice and essay questions. You might think that law school would prepare you for that exam. You would be wrong.

After dropping $125,000 in tuition and spending three years learning at Harvard Law School, I knew maybe 10 percent of the information needed to pass the bar exam. June and July 2002 were all about studying things like commercial paper (a fancy word for checks) and oil and gas law (because I was taking the Texas state bar). It was a grueling two months...but at least I had my "bar trip" to look forward to—one last vacation after taking the exam but before starting my career.

Two of my law-school friends, my now-wife, and I went to Ireland for our bar trip. We had found an online deal that included airfare and the ability to get two rooms per night in the bed-and-breakfasts associated with the travel company. After a brief stay in Dublin, we drove through the beautiful Irish countryside. Every morning we woke up and ate at a bed-and-breakfast, then got in the car and drove to wherever we were going to stay next, enjoying the scenery and not having to read law books.

Well, three of us enjoyed the stunning views we had from our car windows…

My friend John was another story. He slept pretty much *the entire time* we were driving. (The only exception was when we would randomly wake up and yell "Keep left!" to remind the driver to stay on the left side of the road!) I still chuckle at the idea of John sleeping his way through Ireland because, when you're cruising through scenic countryside like that, the journey is kinda the whole point!

EMAIL MARKETING IS THE JOURNEY, NOT THE DESTINATION

One of the biggest struggles for email marketers is that they are like my buddy John—they think of email marketing as the destination, not the journey. And just like John, they end up missing out on a ton. When you think of email marketing as the journey instead of a destination, however, you get a ton of value along the way…and, *oh, by the way*, you also make more sales.

As much as I hear people worrying that they might be bothering their people by emailing them too often, I'm gonna go out on the world's shortest limb and say that's *not* your problem. Why am I so confident in making that prediction? Simple… the problem most people make isn't emailing too often. Heck, when you do email right, your people will *want* to hear from you more often.

The problem most people make is ignoring or ghosting people *except* when they're selling, when suddenly they'll bombard subscribers with a bunch of sales emails. When I randomly start getting emails from someone I haven't heard from in six months, I pretty much know they're coming for my wallet.

How do you think that approach works? If the only time your audience hears from you is when you're selling, expect your emails to be ignored. I mean, who the hell likes it when people only show up when they need something? If you only email people when you're selling stuff, you're positioning yourself as an *askhole*. You give zero value. Instead of being someone who is giving, you are someone who only asks.

People always ask me, "How many emails do I have to send before I try to sell?" And my answer is *always* "I don't know."

I can't give you a rule or a formula or tell you the cheat code to unlocking the exact magic number of emails.[62] There isn't a mathematical equation to give you this answer. In some sense, asking that question is as ridiculous as asking, "What's the meaning of the universe?" in *The Hitchhiker's Guide to the Galaxy*. If you ask a question like that, you'll probably get an answer that makes no sense, like "42."

If you're saying, "How many emails do I *have to* send before I can get to the selling?" you're still stuck in a transactional mindset, fixated on the results. Instead, focus on serving, connecting, and having the chance to change people's lives. You *get* to write

---

62. If there *were* a cheat code, everyone my age would know that it's up, up, down, down, left, right, left, right, B, A, start. If you get this reference, you are *soooooooo* my people.

emails to these people, who are *your people*! They're your friends, the people you serve.

If you fall into the trap of thinking of email as being about the destination (a.k.a. selling) instead of the journey your customers are on, your email marketing is doomed to fail. People will learn to ignore your emails and will tend to unsubscribe in droves.

Magic happens when you take people on a journey instead. When you take people on a journey, they will get to know you, which is a good thing for your business (unless you are a truly horrible person).[63] Taking people on a journey builds the know, like, and trust factor and will position you as a trusted friend who will steer them the right way along this journey you're all on together. (Wow…it's almost like Part I was full of important ideas!)

YOUR ROADMAP OF WHAT'S TO COME IN PART II

The tactical pieces that I'm going to spell out over the next five chapters are designed strategically to take you on a five-step journey to writing emails that help your subscribers trust you.

In building the know, like, and trust factor, we're actually going to start with *trust* first, which may seem weird. But unless people feel like you are an authority, they're just going to tune out. When you start, you're just some random person on the internet to them—and there are *a lot* of random people on the internet. So right up front, you want your subscribers to see you as someone who can truly help them.

---

63. If you *are* a truly horrible person…maybe start by working on that instead of reading a book about email marketing???

Once they're convinced that you can help them, and they trust you, then they will be interested in getting to know you better and like you more.

So the very first email you send and the "nurture sequence," the topics of Chapters 6 and 7, are designed to build that trust and authority.

From there, you shift to the know and like with your welcome sequence, covered in Chapter 8. These emails still help build authority, but they start to focus more on you and less on your subscribers. People can start to make the decision about whether they like you, or if you're not their cup of tea.

You cement the deal in your weekly emails, which you'll see in Chapter 9. You continue to be an ongoing presence as someone who is providing value to them.

Finally, in Chapter 10, it's the moment you've been waiting for: a sales sequence designed to help your raving fans solve a problem by buying your solution.

These sequences are designed in a very specific way, for very specific reasons based upon principles of marketing, psychology, and messaging. It's the reality of what makes humans tick, and basically it's what works. It's been proven out. Copywriters who had previously been following more conventional advice shifted to doing it this way. They say that it's unbelievable how this changes what works and what they see happening with their emails.

It comes down to understanding this fundamental concept about what we need to accomplish with the know, like, and trust factor: start with trust and build the other two.

At this point, you might be thinking, "Bobby, this sounds pretty hard and like it will take a lot longer than what I've been doing."

Well, yeah. But if you're reading this book, I'm guessing that what you've been doing isn't really working, is it?

Look, nothing worth doing is easy. That's the reality. If you want an easy button, go to Staples; if you want reality, stick with me.

The beauty of this is that most of this stuff only has to be created once and then you can set it and forget it. You'll have to go back and review it occasionally, but you put in the time up front to create a curated experience. Then it's *there*, running in the background as people are joining your list. You don't have to think about it except for the weekly emails you're writing on an ongoing basis. Just put in the work, the time, and the effort for a long-term payoff.

If you have written some good emails in the past, I'll give you some shortcuts where you can reuse some of those. You don't have to reinvent the wheel. But if your emails have sucked to this point, and you're starting from scratch, that's okay too. Yes, you're going to have to write a lot of emails, but it will be worth it because this is how you build that connection. It's how you get everything we talked about in Part I.

You'll know it's working when people start responding. When they email to ask, "Hey, when are you going to open the cart again? Because I need that, and I don't want to buy it from someone else." When you take the time to build this connection with your audience, so they know, like, and trust you, you have no competition. People aren't even going to think about buying from anyone else. They're going to ask you when they can buy *your* stuff.

That is the magic of connection. By the time you're selling to them, they're already thinking, "I'm in." Then you don't have to sell.

But here's the deal: selling doesn't work without doing the work in all the emails that lead up to that. You can't skip this and just jump to the tactics of how to sell—it won't work.

So read on and see how to make a connection. It all starts by making a good first impression.

CHAPTER 6

STEP ONE: MAKE A GOOD IMPRESSION WITH A CATCH EMAIL

I MOVED TO FORT WORTH, TEXAS, in 2007 because I got a job as a federal prosecutor. We lived on Bailey Avenue, and right on the corner of Bailey and White Settlement Road was a bar...a bar with no windows, and with a sign out front that said "VIPs." It seemed weird to find a strip club sitting right there at the entrance to this nice residential neighborhood. Sure, White Settlement Road was a rather major street with businesses on it, but overall it was a pretty family-friendly place. What was this seedy strip club doing there?

My wife and I were in our late twenties and, at the time, had no kids, so we enjoyed going out, especially to dive bars for beers and fun. Even after I drank one bar out of its cheapest beers (Schlitz and Pabst Blue Ribbon), and even though VIPs was within walking distance of our house, we weren't about to go hang out at a strip club on a Saturday night.

One afternoon about two years after we'd moved to Fort Worth, I was chatting with one of the law students who was interning in the prosecutor's office. When I asked him about his weekend plans, he said, "I'm going to meet some friends over at VIPs."

I gave him a funny look. Seriously? This guy felt comfortable telling me about his strip club exploits?? Okaaay…a drunken bachelor party, perhaps?

Many people have noted that my face is a walking GIF machine since I'm a wee bit expressive, and I must've let on that something sounded funny because he quickly retorted, "You know it's just a dive bar, right?"

For nearly two years, I had incorrectly assumed that this place was a strip club. My wife and I had passed it many times but never set foot inside—despite the fact that we were their ideal target audience. It was actually the kind of bar we would have enjoyed! But because first impressions matter, our local watering hole missed out on our business for two years.

Once we started going there, we loved it. Cheap beer, shuffleboard, and *fantastic* tamales. (What more do you need in life?) Just think—if that intern and I had never had that conversation, that bar would have completely missed out on their perfect customer.

THE GOAL: MAKE A GOOD FIRST IMPRESSION

Most online entrepreneurs are making the same mistake as the bar with no windows: their emails are making a bad first impression on their potential customers.

The first email you send a new subscriber is *a wee bit* import-ant. If that email sucks, chances are that your audience won't be sticking around. That's why nearly everyone who knows anything about email marketing will tell you that you need to write a good first email.

The first email that *most* subscribers will get from you is the one that delivers the freebie that convinced them to sign up for your list.[64] Most people send a freebie-delivery email that says little more than "here's your stuff." It may be a little bit longer, but it's rarely more than delivering the freebie and telling the new subscriber that you might be sending some more emails later. That's it.

The "here's your stuff" approach is bad on so many levels. To start, your freebie-delivery email is incredibly valuable real estate because that is the *most read* email you ever send ('cause, you know, people want their free thing and all). Wasting your freebie-delivery email is like owning a billboard in Times Square but leaving it blank!

But it gets worse. A boring freebie email isn't just wasting a chance to make a good first impression; it's actively making a *bad* first impression. When people get a bad first impression of your email—whether it's that you're boring or just writing the same old, same old—you're sending the message that you aren't someone who is worth listening to. And let's be honest: since all they really wanted in the first place was the freebie, a boring first email means they'll never come back to read any future emails (and will probably just unsubscribe).

---

64. Once your emails don't suck, you might just have some people who sign up just to get your emails…but that is *not* the norm.

When you write a meaningful first email to subscribers, on the other hand, you start the process of connecting with them. You establish yourself as an **authority** who *is* worth paying attention to. This one little shift can change you from just another random person on the internet to someone who has the answers. Instead of getting the freebie and bouncing, people are going to get that freebie and *stick around*.[65]

Bobby Ruins Marketing

A lot of marketers think they're going to get people on their list and then immediately get those people to buy their premium offers—probably because they heard someone saying they're just "one funnel away" or some such nonsense. Good luck with *that*.

Most people aren't going to join your list and immediately be ready to buy. If people *are* ready to buy your expensive product, they'll just buy it without joining your list separately (happens to me all the time).

If you want to get people to buy expensive products right after joining your list, you're going to have to use hard-sell tactics. Those tactics can make some sales, but using them is penny-wise and pound-foolish. People generally don't like the experience when they're on the receiving end of these tactics, so you are

---

65. Now before you get your hopes up: a good number of people are still going to get the freebie and unsubscribe, no matter what you do. That's the nature of the beast. So don't write me hate mail when some people unsubscribe even after you start sending amazeballs freebie-delivery emails.

losing people who don't buy right away. You lose that potential customer forever, and they might even warn other people away from you.

Feel free to try the hard-sell tactics that the funnel gurus are pushing...I'll be here waiting when that shit doesn't work and you want to learn how to market the right way.

HOOK YOUR SUBSCRIBERS

As much as I make fun of copywriters, one thing I did learn from my copywriter friends is this: the purpose of any line of copy, like a headline, is just to get people to read the next line. In other words, don't try to do *too much* with any single part of the copy you're writing. The goal is just to move them to the next step.

That's actually some profound advice, and we can apply it more broadly when thinking about the goal for each email or email sequence we write. The goal of the first email isn't to move mountains; the goal is to get your subscribers to open the next email. That's it.

In the beginning, you're working to train your subscribers to believe that your emails are valuable or helpful, that they're going to get something out of every single one, so they should always be opening.[66] Kind of like the classic scene from *The Office* where Jim trained Dwight to crave an Altoid anytime he heard a Windows reboot chime—you want your audience members to salivate when they see your name in their inbox.

---

66. It's the exact opposite of selling, which is "always be closing"!

There's a bit of a catch, though. At this point, people are not exactly your biggest fans, so they aren't going to have a ton of patience with you. In other words, you probably can't come in hot with this first email and expect great results. The goal of this first email is to build trust.

This most definitely doesn't mean you're going to spend the whole email bragging about your credentials (which are surely crazy awesome). That's not a good first impression either. At the beginning, people don't give a shit about you. They only care about themselves. You build trust by making them believe that they should care about you.

Ultimately, you want your new subscribers to walk away from that first email thinking, "Wow, Bobby is *in my head*! He must really know what he's talking about."[67] And you're going to do that using the CATCH Structure.

THE CATCH STRUCTURE

At various points, I've heard people say things like "You've got to send a first email that has *feeling*" or "Your first email shouldn't be boring." And others had catchy names for these emails.

That's great and all, but what the hell does that even mean? And more importantly, *how do you actually do that*?

Catchy names and general advice are worthless. What really matters is a repeatable framework that explains how to do the work. Unfortunately, I never did find a framework for that...

---

67. My stick-in-the-mud editor insists that I point out that you should replace "Bobby" with your name and replace the gender-specific pronouns with your pronouns of choice. I thought that was obvious, but my editor is a stickler for these things.

so I came up with one. I thought through what we're trying to accomplish with that first email, pulled in some basic principles of human psychology, and then came up with my CATCH Structure for that first email.[68]

This is a simple, repeatable structure you should use for the first email you send to a new subscriber (whether delivering a freebie or otherwise), and it looks like this:

C: Congratulate Them
A: Acknowledge Their Struggle
T: Tells Me about You
C: Credibility Boost
H: Hook to the Next Email

This email should not be a novel. It's your first email, so keep it on the shorter side. Some of these pieces are only a line or two long. The longest part should be acknowledging their struggle because this email should mostly be about *them*, not you.

Let's break down each piece of the CATCH Structure.

C: Congratulate Them

The first section of the email is to congratulate them. (Or you can call it "Celebrate Them." They both start with C.)

Congratulate your new reader on making the decision to take this step. "Hey, congrats on grabbing your free copy of

---

68. I'm not against catchy names; just make sure they mean something!

[whatever]!" Or "Woohoo! Congratulations on taking action and downloading your freebie!" This should be pretty easy because you are literally congratulating them on *what they've just done.*

Do not underestimate the importance of this step. The only thing you know about this person is that they've grabbed your freebie (or otherwise joined your list). That means the rest of this email is *based upon that one fact,* so you want to make a big deal about them doing it.

Writing this section is simple: some kind of "congrats" line followed by a link where they can download the freebie.

A: Acknowledge Their Struggle

There's a concept in copywriting terms known as agitating the pain. That doesn't mean literally poking your readers or physically hurting them. You're talking about the pain they already have or acknowledging their current struggle. This section is often about a mistake they're making or a belief they have that needs to shift.

Agitating the pain is an incredibly powerful tool because this is what leaves people feeling like you are inside their head. When you can crystallize their struggles and put them into words, your subscribers will automatically see you as an authority. I mean, if you can describe the pain points, surely you can help them solve the problem!

In the CATCH email for people who download one of my core freebies about the "legal stuff" in their business (and you'll see another example at the end of this section), I acknowledge that building an online business is full of a lot of sexy stuff—cool software, six-figure launches, social media, and all that good stuff—but the reality of business is not actually about that.

Here's the Acknowledge Their Struggle section of that CATCH email:

I wanted to take a second to get honest with you.

Online marketing is full of sexy stuff...

Like that new online software that's gonna solve every problem you've thought of... and 157 you didn't know you had!

And we hear all about six-figure launches and the latest social media hacks.

We all love the sexy stuff, but I'm gonna share some #truthbombs with you...

- There's no "silver bullet" when it comes to software... people succeed (and fail) using every software solution under the sun.

- Six-figure launches don't come overnight and you shouldn't trust anyone who says different.

- And Khloe Kardashian's baby is pretty much always going to have more followers than you or me.

With that section of the email, I'm getting them to recognize that this is going to be hard. By introducing the concept of "people who succeed," I'm describing who they want to be. I'm giving them a roadmap to where they want to go and telling them that they have to make this shift. I'm also describing their struggle and things that may be hard for them in a way that resonates with them. Then, subconsciously, they think, "Wow, Bobby is in my head! He *gets* me. And if he gets my struggle, I bet he knows how to solve it."

Bobby's Swift Kick in the Ass

A lot of people tell me that they struggle with writing the section acknowledging their subscribers' struggles. It can be difficult, but only if you haven't done the work to truly understand your people's pain points.

If you can't put your audience's pain points into words and describe their problem, your problem is not with email writing or email marketing. Your problem is that you need to step back and find a way to understand that problem on a fundamental level. If you can't explain what your people are struggling with and how they feel, you're not going to be able to connect with them—and you're gonna have a tough time selling to them.

And this is true throughout all parts of your marketing and business. If you don't truly, deeply understand their problem, how can you explain how your solution *solves that problem*? The answer is: you can't. If you don't know their struggles, your solution won't solve it.

Take the time to understand your people before you ever think about creating a product. There may be an easy button for office supplies, but there isn't one for marketing.

Acknowledging their struggle and talking about their problems or their pain crystallizes the bad news. But then you shift gears into the next section—and it's the good news.

T: Tells Me About You

In the third section of the CATCH email—Tells Me About You—you basically say, "You took the action of downloading the freebie, and *that tells me* that you're going to be among the successful people."

By downloading that freebie (which has to solve that struggle you talked about), they are showing that they have the right mindset and they're taking the right steps.

For the Tells Me About You section of my CATCH email, I highlight that the decision to download a freebie about the legal stuff tells me that the new subscriber is bound to succeed because they're dealing with the *non-sexy* stuff in business. Here's that portion of the email:

You have the secret to long-term success as an online marketer...

...and it has NOTHING to do with the sexy stuff.

Successful entrepreneurs KNOW that to succeed they are going to have to do the sexy stuff... and the non-sexy stuff!

(continued on page 122)

(continued from page 121)

There's no doubt you, Jillian, are among the few who gets it.

You clearly aren't shying away from the non-sexy stuff... I mean, you just grabbed a privacy policy template because you care about the "legal stuff."

Successful entrepreneurs also AREN'T AFRAID to put in the work to get 💩 done.

Taking it slow and bootstrapping ain't bad.

We all dream of getting past the point of bootstrapping (especially the non-sexy stuff), but there's no shame in doing it yourself.

Grabbing my privacy policy template tells me you aren't afraid of a little bootstrapping either.

This section of your email is you telling your readers that downloading your freebie is an important first step because it shows they are on the path to success. Not only does that make them feel good, but it also tells them that following you was a good idea.

Still with me? Awesome. At this point, you're more than 75 percent done with your CATCH email!

C: Credibility Boost

The next section in your CATCH email—Credibility Boost— should be a sentence or two that boosts your credibility. Why are you *the* person they should follow for this information? You can do this with your credentials or your experience, but this is where you should start to weave in your brand voice.

In my email, I say:

> Luckily, you've found a guide for the "legal stuff" who ain't half bad…
>
> …if you're into beer-brewing, jargon-free, slightly irreverent lawyers who use poop emojis and pop-culture references, that is.
>
> …and if you're into more traditional things… like a lawyer who graduated with honors from Harvard Law School, was mentored by a future Supreme Court justice, and worked at elite law firms. (All me, BTW.)
>
> I guess some people are into those kinds of things… whatevs!

My credentials are in there, but I snuck them in while being self-deprecating and letting new subscribers know that I'm not just going to be some boring lawyer, because that's not something they want.

H: Hook to the Next Email

The last section in the CATCH email—Hook to the Next Email—gives readers a sense of what email they're getting next. It makes them excited to read it. (And, oh, by the way, you've seen something like this segue at the end of every chapter in this book!)

The next email will be the first email of your "nurture sequence" (which we'll look at in the next chapter). You should use a curiosity-inducing hook to make sure they are salivating to open that email.

My hook is one-sentence long, and it says, "In my next email, I've got a truly shocking confession to make…"

Let me tell you: people want to know what happens next!

Sometimes you may not know exactly what email comes next; this is normal when writing your first CATCH email. Obviously, to write a hook, you need to know what your next email is going to be. But don't let that stop you from creating your first CATCH email. For now, just leave off the hook. Once you have everything else done, you can go back and add that hook to segue to the next email.

Bobby Ruins Marketing

As long as you're doing these things—speaking to your subscribers' pain points, using their language, and establishing yourself as an authority—I'm not going to be mad if you add something or alter the structure slightly because that works better for you. The point is just to have a structure and to put some thought into the impression you're creating. Most people approach this haphazardly. But once you've learned the rules, break the rules! Hell, I've been breaking the rules of grammar since 1996!

A CATCH Email in Action

Let's look at an example of a complete CATCH email. This is the one people got when they signed up for a quiz about email marketing:

From: Bobby Klinck

Subject: Email Marketing Map [YOUR CUSTOM REPORT]

Hey, Jillian!

Congrats on taking the time to complete the Email Marketing Map Assessment!

Click Here To Download Your Custom Report

Taking the time to dial in your email marketing is a BIG FREAKING DEAL!

Why is it such a big deal? Because it's not the norm.

Let me explain…

Email marketing isn't exactly the "sexy" new thing.

(Understatement of the year!)

Email marketing is the opposite of sexy these days… gurus have been pronouncing it dead for the better part of a decade.

Well, I'm here to tell you that the rumors of email marketing's death have been greatly exaggerated.

(continued on page 126)

(continued from page 125)

Email isn't dead… people are just **doing it wrong**.

Entrepreneurs who're sending their list a boring-ass "newsletter" that just summarizes their content are doing it wrong…

Entrepreneurs who ignore their subscribers until promo time **are doing it wrong…**

Entrepreneurs who are looking for a one-size-fits-all approach to email **are doing it wrong…**

Entrepreneurs who think they can get mad-libs style email templates where all they have to do is plug in a few words **are doing it wrong…**

And I could go on.

Bad email marketing has become an epidemic!

That's the bad news…

But there's a silver lining too!

Because most entrepreneurs just plain suck at email, people who are actually good at it have a leg up.

In a world where subscribers are used to getting boring-ass emails, **emails that aren't boring and that have the right goal stand out.**

Because you took the time to take the Email Marketing Map Assessment (and because you're reading this email), I know one thing about you, Jillian.

You're one of those people whose emails will stand out from the crowd!

No, seriously. Even if you are completely at a loss right now.

How can I make this bold prediction?

(continued on page 127)

(continued from page 126)

Simple.

You took the time to take the assessment.

The reality is that in a world where most people are ignoring email… you're not.

You're ready to actually put in the work — and THAT tells me you're on the cusp of crushing your email marketing goals.

In this world of shitty email marketing, people who are willing to work on getting better absolutely can excel… especially if they have the right person to guide them.

And the really good news for you is that you've found a guide who ain't half bad. 😎

I've built a thriving, multiple-six-figure business selling the most boring thing ever (legal templates) — *using email*.

And in the process, my emails have built a cult following.

Subscribers regularly tell me that my emails are **the only ones** they read…

…copywriters on my list regularly tell me that they have a "Bobby swipe file," where they've collected my emails for future references…

And a big-name copywriter introduced me on his podcast by saying that I write some of the best marketing emails in the biz. 😲

Even better news?

I'm an open book… who's ready to help you **make email marketing one of your superpowers, too!**

The first step is to **click here to download your report and dive into it**!

(continued on page 128)

(continued from page 127)

In my next email, I'm going to tell you about the most ridiculous thing someone ever said about me!

Talk later.

Bobby

With your CATCH email, you've made a big deal of your reader's decision to download whatever you're giving away. You've spoken their language. You've put their pain, their struggles, into words. You've told them that they're on the path to success because they downloaded your giveaway. You've given them some sense of why they should be listening to you. And then you've made them want to read the next email.

When you've done all that, you can see how you're starting to build the trust factor. They trust you. And you're positioning yourself as the authority who can help them with this problem they have. Now they're thinking, "Well, I probably want to listen to this guy."

When you've accomplished that, there's an opening. Now all you have to do is make sure you end up being useful...unlike that advanced physics I learned in school.

CHAPTER 7

STEP TWO:
GET THEM INTO ACTION
WITH A NURTURE SEQUENCE

IN HIGH SCHOOL, I loved physics. Unlike most science classes, which were about memorizing a bunch of made-up-sounding words, physics was my cup of tea because it was about math and logic. My senior year, I took the AP physics class at my school and ultimately ended up with eight hours of college credit after taking the physics subject-matter test on the SAT II. In college, my humanities program required me to take a specific physics class, which meant I was only one hour short of a *minor* in physics, even though I was a liberal arts major.

After all that, sitting here today, I couldn't tell you a single equation I learned, much less the difference between force and momentum. I remember none of it, not because it was boring but because it's just not something I use in my everyday life. As cool as those physics classes were, they have zero value to me, so I don't remember them.

Debate, on the other hand, is something I remember well. I learned to debate as a sophomore in high school and ended up being the Texas state champion my senior year. It's now more than twenty-five years after that debate championship, but I remember plenty. I remember my debate coach's name,[69] the topic we were debating all through the state championship, and random things like Immanuel Kant's categorical imperative and John Rawls's theory of justice.

Why do I remember all those things about debate? It's not because I won the state title; it's because the skills I learned in debate are skills I still use to this day. Debate is how I learned to present an argument, something that carried through to my days as a lawyer. Debate is where I honed my skills as a public speaker, skills that I use regularly in my marketing. Debate is where I learned to spot and deconstruct flaws in other people's arguments, a skill that carries through to my snarky approach to pointing out that everything you think you know is probably wrong!

THE GOAL: GET THEM INTO ACTION

Most entrepreneurs are making a mistake that relegates them to the status of my high school physics class: they are making themselves utterly forgettable because they aren't making sure their people actually use the information in the freebies they download.

---

69. Hey, Mr. Sarabando!

In case you haven't heard, there is some research that suggests that humans have attention spans shorter than that of a goldfish. That has some real consequences for your marketing generally and email marketing more specifically. If you don't capture someone's attention quickly and *make* yourself memorable, you will be forgotten. Hopefully it goes without saying that being forgotten is bad for business.

If someone signs up for one of your free lead magnets but doesn't get value from it (or doesn't even open it), chances are pretty good that you'll be forgotten.

That would be bad.

If you want your people to remember you (hint: you do), you need them to actually use the information in your freebie. While that won't guarantee that they'll stick around and buy from you… it at least gives you a fighting chance.

Let me be brutally honest with you: most people who download your freebie are not going to get value from it *no matter what* you do. I'm guilty of being one of those people in many cases. I jokingly say that my inbox is where freebies go to die. A sizable portion of the people who download your freebie will never use it. Hell, some won't even download it! This chapter isn't about those people.

This chapter is about serving the people who *might* use your freebie if you were to just give them a nudge. Now that you've gotten people onto your list and started the process of establishing credibility with your CATCH email, your goal shifts to making yourself as memorable as my debate class.

So how do you make yourself memorable for your subscribers?

Don't worry; I'm not going to say you have to jump up and down, dance, make videos pointing at nonexistent words or use any other carnival-barker-like techniques. Nope, instead, you're going to create a nurture sequence: a series of emails that will help get your people into action and get them results.

Let's take a look at how to craft a compelling nurture sequence.

WRITING A COMPELLING NURTURE SEQUENCE

Let's talk the nuts and bolts of how to construct a nurture sequence. Unlike the CATCH Structure, there is no *single* structure for your nurture sequence. Instead, you'll need to craft a sequence that makes sense for the specific freebie.

There are a couple of approaches that tend to work well for nurture sequences.

Approach One: Get Your Ass in Gear

Oftentimes, people just need a swift kick in the ass to remind them to take action on the freebie they just downloaded. If you suspect that's what your audience needs, sending one or two emails that encourage them to actually open and use your freebie may be all you need for your nurture sequence.

Here's an example I used for a long time after someone downloaded my free privacy policy legal template:

From: Bobby Klinck

Subject: "Stop buying freaking planners!"

I've got what my wife calls a "planner addiction." On my desk at the moment, I have all of the following:

- The Freedom Journal

- The Mastery Journal

- Full Focus Planner

- The 90x Planner

- At-A-Glance Monthly Planner

It's gotten so bad that my wife has actually banned me from buying any more planners.

(Seriously, I'm a bit scared she'd throw me out and change the locks if I bought any other planners!)

And here's the thing... she's right to be annoyed with my planner addiction.

No, not because planners are bad, but because I don't use *any* of them.

That's right. I've got all these fancy planners that I'm getting zero value from because they are sitting on my shelf unused.

Bad Bobby!

As you can probably guess, though, this isn't really an email about planners...

(continued on page 134)

(continued from page 133)

…I'm writing to make sure you get some value out of the Website Privacy Policy you downloaded recently.

All the fancy legal templates in the world won't protect you *if you don't use them*.

So just wanted to check in to make sure you've put that privacy policy to use!

Do me a favor, if you've customized it and added it to your website, shoot me an email letting me know. You can say anything you want in the email… just let me know you've done it.

If you haven't quite gotten around to it yet, how about we do that now?

Seriously, go find the email the system sent with your login credentials and go get that baby done now.

Think about it this way… the sooner you get legal policies in place, the sooner you can quit thinking about the "legal stuff."

Here's betting that's something that sounds pretty good to you.

That's it for now… I'm gonna go stare longingly at my planner collection now.

Talk later.

Bobby

P.S. And once you've customized the Privacy Policy and realized how easy it is to use, don't forget you can grab the other two templates you need to fully protect your website for just $97. If you're ready to get your website 100% protected, <u>click here and grab the Website Legal Policy Pack</u>.

The get-your-ass-in-gear email is particularly useful for freebies like my privacy policy—freebies that are all about executing. If you offer a tool or template freebie, you generally don't need to give people any more information to get full value; you just need to give them that kick in the ass to take action.

Approach Two: The Entertaining Education Sequence

When your freebie isn't something as self-executing as a template or tool, you'll probably need something more than a simple kick-in-the-ass email for your nurture sequence. This is where you'll use a multi-email educational sequence.

The length of this sequence will be tied to the freebie your new subscriber just downloaded. As a general rule of thumb, you'll send one email per topic or step in the freebie. The nurture sequence for my "Ultimate Legal Checklist" is a good example. It is five emails long, with an email each about (1) trademark issues, (2) copyright issues, (3) privacy issues, (4) website legal policies, and (5) getting agreements in writing.[70] These emails go out one day apart so I'm constantly in front of my new audience, providing value and staying top of mind.

In each of the nurture emails you send, you'll either go a bit deeper than you did in the freebie or provide more context around the topic. The exact content doesn't really matter so long as it's useful and not completely repetitive of what's in the freebie itself. The goal here is to simply get in front of your audience multiple times to

---

70. The freebie covers one other topic—creating an LLC. We decided not to cover that in the email sequence because it might bore people to tears.

drive home the importance of what you're teaching. Getting multiple emails from you will encourage them to open the freebie and get into action. But even if they never open the freebie, the emails should help them take action, which will make you memorable!

Although you are educating your audience, you have to remember the whole "attention span of a goldfish" thing. That means you have to teach in an entertaining way.[71] While I'm not sure there's ever a good time to be boring, this is most definitely *not* the time to be boring.

By way of example, here are the subject lines of the emails in that legal checklist nurture sequence:

- Which of these is the worst brand name?

- And He is testing us!

- Why do I always forget to go incognito?

- I have a confession to make...

- The MOST obvious legal mistake in the world...and I made it

Each of the emails tells a quick story of me screwing something up before pivoting to the legal lesson.

But keep in mind that in the nurture sequence, your readers haven't yet warmed up to you. At this point, you're still talking

---

71. Kind of like how *The Good Place* taught a lot of people the basics of moral philosophy in the context of an entertaining television show.

about them and helping them solve a problem. They don't really even *know* you yet, other than what they may have read in the CATCH email. In your nurture emails, you should keep your stories short, as compared to the content that follows.

Here's one of those emails from my sequence as an example:

From: Bobby Klinck

Subject: Why do I always forget to go incognito?

If there's one rule we ALL need to remember it's to use an incognito window in Chrome when we are doing any sensitive web browser.

Unfortunately, that's a rule that I pretty much never remember… and it can lead to some uncomfortable situations.

Like the time my wife looked over at me recently and said:

> "Why am I seeing ads for dating sites and erectile dysfunction pills on your Facebook? Is there something I should know???"

Like I said… uncomfortable situations.

Luckily for me, there is ALWAYS a reasonable explanation. Okay, maybe not reasonable… but definitely a non-guilty explanation!

In that case, the trouble was that I had been doing some market research for work I was doing with a couple of my business coaching clients.

(continued on page 138)

(continued from page 137)

After I explained the situation, my wife rolled her eyes and went on with her day.

(FYI... that's a rather common occurrence in my household!)

One of these days, I swear that I'll remember to go incognito.

Now that you've had your daily dose of dumb stuff Bobby has done... time for a quick legal lesson.

Today's lesson is part legal and part marketing... we're talking about privacy.

For much of the past decade, online marketing has been built on the idea of using other people's data to tailor just about everything when it comes to their online experience.

That's why those sneakers you put in your cart but didn't buy follow you around the internet (in the form of ads)... and why my FB feed is full of ads for products directed at online marketers.

As someone who remembers the endless pop-ups and banner ads of the early internet, I'm ALL for targeted ads...

...but we online marketers are kinda in the minority on this.

Most of our potential customers get creeped out about the level of targeting that's happening.

And as a result, we've seen a wave of laws that are all about protecting people's privacy.

When I was thinking about how to explain privacy in this email, I was reminded of Inigo Montoya's quote in *The Princess Bride*:

"Let me explain... No, there is too much. Let me sum up."

(continued on page 139)

(continued from page 138)

Seriously, digging into the details of the GDPR, the Cookie Directive, and the CCPA (just 3 of the relevant laws) would take an entire book.

But assuming you are not an arsehole (i.e., you're not trying to be shady), there are really two rules you need to follow.

First, be transparent about what you do.

One of the central ideas of the new privacy laws is that people should KNOW what you are doing with their data.

This idea isn't really surprising because legal nerds like me have always loved this now more than a century-old quote from Supreme Court Justice Louis Brandeis: "Sunlight is said to be the best of disinfectants."

In other words… exposing what people are doing is one of the best ways to encourage good behavior.

Applying this to your business, it means doing things like:

- ☑ Telling people what information you collect, why you collect it, what you'll do with it, and who you'll share it with.

- ☑ Including a Cookie Notice on your website so people know that you are using tracking cookies.

- ☑ Telling people if you sell personal data that you collect.

You'll generally do these things through things like privacy policies, cookie notices, and other disclaimers.

But don't just hide this in your wordy legal policy… cause, you know, transparency!

Be clear with people about what you'll be doing with their data.

(continued on page 140)

(continued from page 139)

Aside from keeping you on the right side of the law, it's also good marketing.

Second, give people the power to choose.

The privacy regulations are built on the idea that people should be given the choice about how their data is used.

CAN-SPAM requires that you allow people to opt-out of your emails.

The GDPR generally requires that you get consent to use information you collect for marketing.

The CCPA provides that people have the right to opt out of certain things you might do with their data.

You get the point... Let people choose.

All the transparency in the world isn't worth much if people can't do something with what you tell them.

So let people easily opt out of your email list.

Make it easy for people to delete all their data from your systems.

We are permission-based marketers, so we should act like it.

With privacy issues, it's kind of funny... complying with the law is largely about being a decent human being!

So go be decent.

In my next email, I have an important confession to make... and I'll share a free resource to comply with the privacy rules (FYI - it's actually the ONLY legal policy or document that you're required to have!).

Talk later.

Bobby

As you can see, probably three quarters of the email is the lesson itself. The story is used just as a quick hook to get people interested.

CAN YOU SELL IN YOUR NURTURE SEQUENCE?

A lot of entrepreneurs want to go straight for a sale after someone downloads a freebie. Generally, this would be for a lower-priced product, but it is a sale nonetheless. While this approach *can* work, it is not my preferred approach. Sales-based nurture sequences are truly polarizing (and not in the good way). They will get some people to buy, but they will tend to turn off a lot of the people who join your list and who might have been valuable long-term customers.

When you send nurture emails that are *not* trying to sell anything, just trying to get them to take action, people will be *stunned*. "You're not trying to make me buy anything?!" This will establish you as a trusted advisor, as someone who is more of a friend—not some rando on the internet who comes across as a sleazy salesperson. Choosing not to sell up front sets you apart from most other people out there... and that makes you memorable.[72]

But in order to *really* seal the deal, you also need to tell them who you are and what you can do for them. Buckle up; that's ahead in Chapter 8.

---

72. If you choose to disregard my guidance, keep any up-front sales sequences short and sweet.

CHAPTER 8

STEP THREE: GIVE THEM THE ABCs OF *YOU* WITH A WELCOME SEQUENCE

AFTER WE HAD BEEN TOGETHER FOR ALMOST TWENTY years, my wife turned to me one afternoon and asked, "Why do you look at the sun when you want to sneeze?"

The question perplexed me. I mean, the answer seemed so obvious: because looking at the sun makes you sneeze.

Well, it turns out the answer was not so obvious…

My wife explained that looking at the sun doesn't make her sneeze, not even a little, but she had noticed that our daughter also sneezes when she looks at the sun. So she was trying to understand.

The whole conversation was surreal. I had spent my whole life believing that the sun made everyone sneeze. My wife, on the other hand, just thought I was weird.[73]

A brief search on the Google proved that I am weird...or at least in the minority. The reflex to sneeze because of bright light (and especially the sun) is called the "photic sneeze reflex." It's a genetic quirk shared by around 20 percent of the population.

My wife and I had both spent more than thirty-five years of our lives having no idea how the other side lived. And it turns out that complete ignorance of the other side is common when it comes to the photic sneeze reflex. After chatting with my parents, I discovered that my mom had never heard of such a thing until she married my dad...and, like me, he had no idea that he was weird.

And I never would have known if my wife hadn't asked that simple question.

THE GOAL: POSITION YOURSELF AND YOUR BUSINESS

While my wife being in the dark about my photic sneeze reflex makes for a good story, here's what's not so funny: there's a good chance that your audience is equally in the dark about key parts of your business. You have to be proactive about solving this problem.

Think of it this way: I'm a pretty big part of my wife's life, and it still took her *twenty years* to ask about the whole sneezing

---

73. In her defense, that's always a safe assumption.

thing. And she only asked because our daughter seemed to have the same weird trait. How likely do you think it is that your audience will *ever* ask about the things they don't know about your business?

Let me humbly suggest that instead of waiting for them to ask, you should just go ahead and *tell* your audience about the important parts of your business. Give them an introduction to who you are, an orientation to your world, and make it clear how you can help them.

In marketing, there's a concept known as positioning. In a nutshell, positioning is about occupying a specific space in your customer's mind. Your audience needs to understand exactly how you can help them solve their problems, whether through free content or paid products. Just as importantly, they need to understand what makes you different from your competitors. As someone selling your knowledge and expertise, that's largely about *you* and your approach.

The trouble is that very few online marketers take the time to position themselves. Chances are good that you assume people know all about your business, but usually they don't, because guess what? We're just not that important. As much as you might like your people to think about you all the time, they don't. And that is a real problem.

Rather than waiting for people to ask about your business, you position yourself with your welcome sequence. A welcome sequence is a strategic series of emails used to bring people into your world so they can start to think of you as a solution to a very specific problem.

SET THE TONE TO CONNECT WITH *YOUR* PEOPLE

Your welcome sequence is also about setting the tone so you can cull your audience, right up front. Some of that happens naturally as you tell people about your core values (a.k.a. what your business stands for). For example, if you are going to take political, social, or cultural stands, you might as well do that from the beginning. If someone doesn't want to hear those points of views (or vehemently disagrees with you)...bye-bye!

This is when your emails shift to being more about *you* and *your* personality. If you are a big personality, it's time to let them know.

Here's the email that starts my welcome sequence, so you can see how you might invite people to make the decision of whether they want to stick around:

From: Bobby Klinck

Subject: Buckle up... it's gonna get weird.

Wait... did I just tell you my emails are gonna get weird?

Why the hell would I do something that might convince you to unsubscribe right now instead of ease you into things?

Let me explain with a story.

Back in 1997, when I was in college, I was a HUGE Kevin Smith fan. I mean who didn't love *Clerks* and *Mallrats*?!?!

(continued on page 147)

(continued from page 146)

So I was downright stoked to go see *Chasing Amy* with my girlfriend (who's now my wife!).

When it was over… I was PISSED!

(Not sure if this is necessary for a 23-year-old movie, but a spoiler is coming…)

Who the hell makes a "romantic-comedy" where the guy ***doesn't get the girl.***

I made my wife sit through the closing credits to make sure there wasn't a secret happy ending.

Nope.

We'd been hoodwinked.

And that felt shitty!

That lesson stuck with me, so I want people to know what they're getting themselves into when they join my email list.

It's not that I'm intentionally abrasive or out trying to "be polarizing" like so many marketing gurus are teaching.

It's just that I'm an irreverent kinda guy who sometimes swears and tends to say what he thinks even if it's not gonna be popular.

So lemme give you a preview.

If you stick around, you're going to end up on my list where you get emails telling you about the latest episode of **The Certified BADA$$ Online Marketing Podcast**.

Those emails have gotten a bit of a cult following… and their fair share of haters…

(continued on page 148)

(continued from page 147)

...because they're me in a nutshell—snarky, sometimes shocking, and chocked full of really corny jokes and pop-culture references.

People who are cool with that tend to LOVE my emails because they make them laugh (sometimes WITH me... and sometimes AT me) and deliver nuggets of wisdom to help them build their businesses.

But some people just plain can't take the snark and pop-culture.

The last thing I want is for you to feel the shock I felt at the end of *Chasing Amy*... you should know **exactly what you're getting yourself into.**

So, in the coming weeks, you'll be getting some of my greatest hits...

These are the emails that generated the MOST buzz — positive and negative. Interestingly, they tend to be the same emails.

(Psst... that last sentence might be one of those nuggets of wisdom.)

So buckle up... it's gonna get weird!

Talk later.

Bobby

It's worth highlighting a few things about that email. There's the obvious fact that I tell people what to expect in future emails. But that's just scratching the surface. There are also some meta things going on in the email.

The email starts with a story, like nearly all the emails my audience will get from me. But this is not just any story; it's a story that includes me and my wife *and* includes a pop-culture reference. That story introduces common themes that I use throughout my email marketing—the people who are forced to put up with my crazy antics and pop-culture fanaticism.

Just as importantly, you'll notice that I used the word "shitty." I don't always curse, but I am a firm believer that sometimes a curse word is the best choice. By dropping a single curse in this email, I'm foreshadowing that my emails will sometimes have dirty words in them.

Using the first email of your welcome sequence to set the tone for what is to come—in the welcome sequence and beyond—is a great way to cultivate connection with your audience, which will build raving fans.

LET'S GET TACTICAL: WHAT TO INCLUDE IN YOUR WELCOME SEQUENCE

While there are countless topics you *could* cover in your welcome sequence, there are a few boxes that many (if not most) online marketers should check. Think of these as the core email types for your welcome sequence, and use the ones that apply to your business.

Start with Your Origin Story

Other than an intro email (like the one in the last section), your welcome sequence should start with one or more emails that tell your origin story. There are two types of origin stories.

The "Walking the Same Path" Model

If you are like most online business owners, you are on the same journey as your customers; you're just further along in the journey.

If that's the case, your origin story is simply your story told in a way that will resonate with your audience.

Using this model, great origin stories follow a three-part story arc. Part one describes you in the "hell," suffering from the same pain and frustrations that are plaguing your audience. Part two describes the aha moment where you found a better or different way. Part three describes you in the "heaven," enjoying the results your audience wants.

This story can be told in either one or two emails. If you can truly dig into the pain, this can be done masterfully in two emails. The first email focuses exclusively on the hell. In it, you describe your pain and frustration in depth, using *your audience's* language as much as possible. This first email walks them through the absolute torment you were in and then says something like "But everything changed for me when I discovered one thing…And I'll tell you what that was in my next email."

With that one sentence, you've created the hook. In the next email, you pick up with the change you made, how that affected things, and where you are now.

The Professional Training Path

If you are an expert as a result of special training—instead of simply being ahead of your audience on the journey—your origin story will tend to look a bit different. You likely didn't face the same struggles as your audience, which makes it harder to connect with your audience.

But all is not lost!

If this is your path, tap into *why* you chose to serve the audience you serve. Maybe you didn't personally face the same struggles, but chances are that you were drawn to serve this audience because you saw someone *else* going through the hell. Tapping into this why and describing what makes you passionate about serving this audience is how you bridge the connection gap as an expert.[74]

Got Secondary Freebies?

Do you have any additional freebies that aren't great for getting people in the door but that would really serve your audience?

When I was just "the legal guy," nearly everyone joined my list through my free privacy policy, but I also had a training program called The Online Genius Academy. It was a free online course about the legal stuff for online entrepreneurs. I figured out early on that pitching people who didn't yet know me to take a course about the legal stuff was a nonstarter. Not surprising because, you know, the legal stuff seems pretty boring.

Although people who didn't know me weren't interested in the academy, people already on my list *were* interested. So giving people access to that freebie after they were already on my list was a no-brainer.

Giving people these kinds of secondary freebies is about building up goodwill. *And giving is never a bad thing.*

If you don't have a secondary freebie, don't feel the need to create one. But if you do, you sure as shit should tell your people

---

74. If you aren't passionate about who you serve, there's not much I can do. Well, that's not true…let me not-so-humbly suggest that you *find* an audience you are passionate about serving.

about it. There's nothing fancy about this email. Tell them a story and give them the gift.

Your Core Values

The third type of email is about your core values. Every business should have core values. These are the things you stand for. The things you believe in. Sometimes they are very specific to what you do or teach, and other times they are broader and not as closely related to it.[75] Your core values will often be some of the things that make your business unique, so you should tell your audience about them in your welcome sequence.

One approach is to send a single email that lists all your core values. Alternatively, you could highlight individual core values in stand-alone emails. If you've created a piece of content that explains your core values, send your people to consume that content. Because I have created podcast episodes about multiple of my core values, I include individual values in an email and link out to the different episodes. This gives my subscribers a sense of what I stand for and believe in, which is helping people build a business.

Ultimately, it doesn't matter exactly *how* you tell people your core values; just make sure your audience knows what your values are before leaving your welcome sequence.

---

75. My core values include things like being a radical giver, making business fun, keeping business simple, doing the unscalable, being inclusive, and being authentically me.

Core Content

Sometimes you'll link your core values email with this next type of email, which is about your core content.

In your core content email, you want to tell people about, you guessed it: your core content. If you have a blog, tell them about your blog. If you have a podcast or video channel, tell them about that. Whatever your core content is, you should have at least one email about it.

I tend to combine the core values and core content emails. I tell people about my podcast and then send them to various podcast episodes that are about different core values. That way, people are hearing and experiencing my podcast, but they're also learning my core values.

You can also introduce them to your core content by giving them a curated list of some of your best-ever episodes or posts.

Core Social Media

The topic of the next type of email is your core social media.

I recommend picking one social media platform that you would like people to follow you on and sending them there. In my case, I send people to my Facebook group because I like building community. You might send them to Instagram instead. Wherever you spend the most time and would really like to build up, that's where you should send them. That's a place you can provide value and connect with them, and they can get to know you better. You want them to know about that.

Important Lessons

This is a category of email that you might not have, at least not at the beginning of your email marketing journey. Sometimes you'll have a message or lesson you want to get across to your audience but that doesn't fit into another email type. If you have an important lesson to share, then you'll want to use one of these emails.

One of my most engaged emails of all time falls into this camp. It started as a weekly email but has now become a staple of my welcome sequence:

From: Bobby Klinck

Subject: "They're okay…"

One afternoon, a couple of weeks before the start of my final year in law school, I answered the phone to hear my mom say:

> *"They're okay…"*

Not sure about you, but that's not exactly how I want a conversation to start…

(continued on page 155)

(continued from page 154)

My mom explained that my dad and uncle had been in a plane crash in their private plane.

They'd been taken to the hospital to get checked out... but she stressed that they were okay.

And then my brother called a few hours later... he was the first to get to the hospital.

They weren't okay.

Not at all.

My uncle was burned over 85% of his body and my dad was burned over 45% of his body.

The doctors told my brother they didn't expect my uncle to make it through the night... and that my dad's chances weren't much better.

The next ten weeks of my life are a blur...

Most of that time was spent in a hotel on the military base where my dad was being treated... and where my uncle was treated until he passed away.

The law school was amazingly flexible about things... letting a friend handle my registration for me and telling me to get back when I could.

There was just one little hiccup...

I was **supposed** to be competing in the final round of a prestigious competition that semester (where I'd be one of four Harvard Law students who get to stand and argue a case before federal court judges).

It was the culmination of a year's worth of hard work and achievement.

But I was thinking about bowing out to stay with my family...

(continued on page 156)

(continued from page 155)

…because my dad *still hadn't woken up*.

That's when one of my dad's best friends sat me down and made perfectly clear that there was not a choice to be made. He told me my dad would **expect** me to leave to compete and he'd be pissed when he woke up if I skipped it.

So I competed in the most prestigious legal competition in the country while I had no idea whether my dad would survive…

This isn't a story I talk about a lot, and I'm not telling it to you for sympathy.

I'm telling you this story because the reality is that life is going to knock you down.

Things are gonna get hard.

The timing is never going to be perfect.

Your life and your business are going to have to coexist.

And being successful means finding a way to power through when things are hard.

My dad's plane crash taught me all those lessons in spades.

Because of my dad's friend, I had the honor of standing before three federal court of appeals judges to argue a case… as a freaking student!

Although my team didn't win, one of the biggest name professors at Harvard (noted Supreme Court practitioner Larry Tribe) went out of his way to tell his class that these were the two best teams he could remember in the competition.

I would have missed it all… except that I was **committed**.

You know what?

(continued on page 157)

(continued from page 156)

Successful entrepreneurs are the ones who bring that same commitment to their businesses.

When shit gets hard... they power through.

Today, I don't have a podcast for you to listen to or another freebie to send your way.

My call to action to you is simple:

Commit to yourself that you'll keep going.

Commit to yourself that you'll get back up when your life or business knocks you down.

And if you're willing, **hit REPLY to tell me you're committed.**

It can be as simple as just the word "committed," or as involved as you like.

I'll read that response personally.

My next email won't be a downer, I promise. (These kinds of emails are few and far between... but this was too important of a lesson not to share.)

Talk later.

Bobby

P.S. My dad's story has a happy ending. He woke up a couple days after I headed back to school for the start of the competition, and he was doing well enough a month or so later that my mom was able to come up for a couple of days to see me actually argue the case... and my dad watched parts of it on a livestream. (This was 2001, and the law school honored my request by agreeing to livestream the competition for the first time ever.)

That email is one of the most powerful I've ever written, and it is one that gets more responses than any other. Nearly every Tuesday and Friday (more on that timing in an upcoming section), I get at least one email landing in my inbox with a simple line: "Committed."

If you have a powerful lesson to share…share it.

Core Products

The final type of email to send is about your core products. This is one or more emails that introduce your people to the core ways you can help them. People should know about all your core products and services, and how they can buy them. Don't leave people guessing about how you can solve their problems; tell them!

If people can buy your products anytime, include an email that expressly invites them to buy. Like, right now. Tell them the details, and give them a link to the sales page where they can learn more about your offers.

If you use a launch method where people can only buy at certain times of the year, these emails should describe your program and let people know when they will be able to buy. You can invite them to join a waitlist in the meantime.

The key point here is to simply tell people how they can give you money.

OPEN AND CLOSE

One of the most important skills I learned in debate (yep, another skill I still use!) is the idea of signposting. It's a simple idea: tell people where you're going to take them, take them there, and then tell them where you've been. My recommendation is to do something similar with your welcome sequence. The guts of your sequence—the core emails we just discussed—are the "take them there" part. But it's helpful to include introduction and conclusion emails.

You already saw my introduction email, the email where I tell people that it's going to get weird (literally the subject line). That's me giving them a taste of what's to come. (And that way, if I'm not for them, if my using four-letter words occasionally is going to bother them, they can go ahead and unsubscribe).

Your conclusion email should just put a bow on things and to let them know what to expect on a weekly basis going forward. Bonus points if it harkens back to the theme from your introductory email.

For me, that means giving them props for being someone who seems to enjoy my particular kind of weird:

From: Bobby Klinck

Subject: Are you still here?

Hey Jillian,

Can you believe it's been almost six weeks since I told you:

"Buckle up… it's gonna get weird."

(continued on page 160)

(continued from page 159)

Time sure does fly when you're having fun.

Since you're still here, I'm guessing that you're one of the people who's attracted to my particular kind of weird…

That's pretty damn cool in my book.

Since you've decided to stick around… you're about to join the other brave souls who've decided they want to hear from me from week-to-week.

You can expect an email every Tuesday with some crazy shenanigans in my life and announcing my newest podcast episode…

…and an email on Fridays inviting you to my Friday Live edition of the podcast (which will normally be a swift kick in the ass).

If you ever need anything from me, just HIT REPLY.

My team handles the basic customer support stuff (because I'd be more likely to break it more than to fix it)… but I'm the one who sees and responds to the other stuff.

I love chatting with entrepreneurs generally, and especially with entrepreneurs who are attracted to my particular kind of weird.

Talk later.

Bobby

You don't *need* to include an introduction or conclusion email, but giving people their footing is always a good idea.

ANSWERS TO SOME COMMON QUESTIONS

People tend to have a lot of questions about the welcome sequence, so here's a lightning round with answers to the most common questions I hear.

"Is there an exact number of emails I should include in my welcome sequence?"
Nope. There is no exact formula. You might opt to not include one of the types of emails listed above, you might choose to include more than one email that covers a particular topic, or you might decide to send a type of email that isn't even listed above. My welcome sequence has been as many as thirteen emails because I really want people to get to know me.

You may send more; you may send fewer. For example, if you don't have a secondary freebie, you're not going to send a secondary freebie email. If you haven't yet created your first product, you probably don't want to highlight that gap by talking about your lack of products. If you haven't figured out the social media aspect of your business yet, you're not going to include an email about the socials.

You get the point. Your welcome sequence should be long enough to highlight the important parts of your business.

"How do I structure these emails?"
Most of these emails will follow that same structure of hook, story, call to action. You have general calls to action throughout—telling readers to follow you, to join the group, or to click over to your page to learn more about your products.

In your core values email, you'll have to come up with a call to action. Because one of my core values is that business should be fun, this could be as simple as asking them to hit reply and tell me about how *their* business is fun.

"How far apart should I send these emails?"

I suggest sending them out twice a week. Most entrepreneurs will fall into a once-a-week pattern for regular emails to their list, so your welcome sequence emails are starting to get more spaced out than the emails that came before but are more frequent than the weekly emails. You don't want to make people wait two or three months before they start receiving your regular weekly emails. And it's balanced between the every-day or every-other-day rhythm of the nurture sequence and the weekly rhythm of your normal list.

The sequence should be set up for emails to go out on the day you'll send your standard weekly email and then about halfway through the week. So, for example, my weekly email has always gone out on Tuesdays, so my welcome sequence emails go out on Tuesdays and Fridays. This approach trains your audience about when to expect emails from you going forward.

"Is this too much about me, me, me? Aren't people going to get sick of reading about me?"

Maybe, but not really. Let's face facts: most people aren't going to read all your emails. And if people *are* reading all your emails, it's a pretty good sign that they want to hear more from you and about you. If people are enjoying your emails, send more of them.

You're talking about how you can provide value, how you can help them. So even though it sounds like "me, me, me" to you, it's not. These emails are about how you can serve your new subscribers; they are providing a roadmap for your audience. You're just sprinkling in a little bit of yourself to build the connection along the way.

"Do I have to write them all from scratch?"
If you are just starting out with email marketing, then obviously you're going to have to write this sequence from scratch. Similarly, if you've really sucked at email up to this point, you should most likely start from a blank slate.

But that won't always be the case. When I revise my welcome sequence these days, it's almost always an exercise in repurposing some of my best weekly emails. If you've got greatest hits (a.k.a. emails that people rave about), include them in your welcome sequence. It would be a real shame for your best stuff to never be seen by new people. You will most likely have to tweak the call to action in these greatest-hits emails, but there's no reason not to repurpose the story.

"How often does your welcome sequence change?"
Your business is a living, breathing thing that will evolve, and your welcome sequence will need to evolve with it. When you introduce a new signature product or introduce a new major content platform, you'll want to revisit your welcome sequence to make sure it's still accurate. The same goes with any new core values or messages.

But there's something else worth noting: you'll also want to revisit your welcome sequence every once in a while to make sure it doesn't include something that hasn't aged well.

One of my all-time-greatest-hits emails included a wild story from my days as a federal prosecutor about the other prosecutors and some ATF agents playing a pretty wicked prank on me—a prank involving the agent telling me there was a barricaded suspect and asking me to authorize the use of deadly force. When I first started sending out this email, people loved it. They thought it was hilarious. It was among my most talked-about emails (in a positive way). One of my copywriter friends even told me it was the best story she had ever read.

But that is a story that has not aged well. As wild as the story was, law enforcement officers asking for permission to use deadly force is not a joking matter. It probably was never funny, but the events of 2020 (including the deaths of George Floyd and so many others) highlighted that fact. It was time to retire that email for good.

While there is no hard-and-fast rule about how often to revisit your emails, you should be aware of major cultural shifts that might warrant a change. Once you have sequences in place, you need to go back and check on them every once in a while to make sure they're not insensitive or simply out of date.

We try to revisit the welcome sequence at least yearly, but it really depends on the pace of your business and the pace of change in your business.

One More Question

The question I get most from people is "Do I have to do the work?" Okay, they don't actually ask me that directly, but a lot of the questions I get asked are basically asking my permission to not do the work.

You have to do the work, but it's worth it. Remember, these are emails that you'll write once but that will go out for months or maybe even years to come (assuming they age well!). Writing these emails is making an investment in your business.

I want to take a moment and really emphasize how important it is that you send a welcome sequence. You *should not skip this part* and just start sending your weekly emails.

I went to the University of Texas at Austin for undergrad. It's a huge campus, so before we even started our first classes, they gave us an orientation. We spent some time walking around so we got to know the lay of the land. That way, when we had to find different buildings, we didn't feel lost and confused.

If you skip sending this welcome sequence, it's like plopping someone right in the middle of that campus with no map, no cell phone, and no guide, and saying, "Meet me at this hall in five minutes." They'll never be able to do it! They'll just wander around, lost and confused, wondering why their so-called friend wants them to feel that way.

But once you've sent your CATCH email, nurture sequence, and welcome sequence, your subscribers are officially part of your world!

We talked generally about your weekly emails in Part I, but Chapter 9 is going to give you more-specific information on how to continue building that connection so that your readers' favorite…is you!

CHAPTER 9

STEP FOUR:
ENGAGE YOUR AUDIENCE
WITH WEEKLY EMAILS

I'VE ALWAYS LOVED TV AND HAVE WATCHED MY SHARE of TV shows from start to finish. I'll never forget Sam Malone turning away a customer to close out the last episode of *Cheers*. And who can forget the four friends walking back to their jail cell at the end of *Seinfeld*? Every ending is different. Some provide closure that seems a fitting end. Others seem abrupt and just plain ruin the entire series.[76] And some are endlessly debated (like what to make of the closing scene of *The Sopranos*).

Regardless of the ending itself, I always felt sad when one of my favorite shows ended. At the time, it seemed that I was sad because there was suddenly a hole in my entertainment schedule.

---

76. I'm looking at you, creators of *Chuck*. What the hell was that?!?

And I always doubted that there would ever be a show I would like as much. When *Cheers* wrapped, I remember thinking there would never be a show that good again.

But I always moved on and found something else to watch…

During the pandemic, I finally figured out why the endings made me sad. I've taken to binging a lot of shows from start to finish: *Schitt's Creek*, *Monk*, *Chuck*, *The Good Place*, and *Psych*, to name a few. When each ended, I had that *same* feeling of sadness and emptiness I'd felt when the shows wrapped up in real time. Not knowing what to watch next had nothing to do with it.

The sadness came from the fact that it felt like my *friends* were leaving me. Over the arc of the shows, I ended up invested in the (fake) lives of the characters. That connection is what TV writers tap into. They've figured out that once you're invested in the life of just one character, you'll keep coming back week after week.

There's an important lesson you can take from that to apply to your email marketing.

THE GOAL: KEEP YOUR AUDIENCE ENGAGED

What TV writers understand is that the key to getting people to come back over and over again is to get them *invested* in the lives of the characters. When we're invested as viewers, we come back each week because we *need* to know what happens in the lives of those characters.

You can probably see where this is going…

The trick to keeping your audience engaged is about getting them *invested* in you and your life. People want to see into your life. If you let them get that glimpse, guess what? They will be addicted to your weekly emails, just like we're all addicted to TV shows. When you combine the power of storytelling with that human instinct to want to see into other people's lives, and you tell stories about yourself and your life, you let people *see you* and *get to know you*. That means they're going to come back, and, as you let them into your world even more, that's what allows them to connect with you.

And they won't want to leave because saying goodbye will leave them with that same empty feeling we all get when our favorite show ends.

You create this ongoing connection with your weekly emails. If you follow the standard advice to send a newsletter that's filled with a lot of substantive content, you won't keep people engaged. If you want to succeed with your weekly emails, you have to provide a reason for people to come back week after week.

These emails should tell stories about you—you as a person, not you as a business owner—to let people in on your life. To keep them coming back. And to take people from casual followers to raving fans who are ready to buy everything you offer.

THE REAL WORLD EFFECT

If you have *any* doubt about the power of story to keep people coming back, the reality TV boom dispelled it. What Mary-Ellis Bunim and Jonathan Murray instinctively knew when they created *The Real World* (the first of the modern reality shows) was that people would feel an even deeper connection to *real* people as opposed to scripted characters.

The rest, as they say, is history. Reality TV has become an ever-growing portion of the programming (especially as a percentage of dramatic programming). People simply cannot get enough of their reality TV, from *The Real Housewives* to *Keeping Up with the Kardashians.* We keep coming back because we simply *have to know* what happens.

Ironically, you'll hear a lot of people talk about reality TV shows in the online space. But the lesson they take from it is wrong. You'll often hear people talk about it in the context of researching your ideal customer avatar, or ICA. One of my more popular weekly emails took issue with the suggestion:

From: Bobby Klinck

Sent: July 23, 2019

Subject: Do you really need to know what magazine your ICA reads?

In early 2018, as part of a course I was in, I took the time to create a really detailed sketch of my ideal customer avatar.

The program pushed me to define things like:

- My ICA's hair color and eye color?

- Where she lives?

- What her favorite TV shows and fiction books are?

- What magazines she reads?

- What her favorite guilty pleasure is?

(continued on page 171)

(continued from page 170)

I did it all, and could describe "Julia" to a tee. Right down to the brown hair, green eyes, and love of Starbucks Mochas.

Heck I even knew that she and her husband John lived in Scranton and had a son named "Simon."

That's right… **I did the work**.

BUT, time for some #BobbyHonesty…

The whole freaking exercise was stupid.

There, I said it.

Before you cast me as a pariah… I'm not saying you shouldn't do ICA work.

I'm just saying that the normal way it's taught is dumb.

Do you really think having a "name" for your ICA or creating a story about their hair color matters?

That sh*t doesn't matter.

But I'm gonna take things one step further… the standard ICA work can be hazardous to your business.

The problem is that focusing on the superficial crap often makes people feel like they've done the work when they haven't.

The ICA work that really matters has nothing to do with hair color or eye color or guilty pleasures.

I mean, if my ICA watches the Real Housewives of whatever… I'm not gonna pretend I like (or even tolerate) those shows to connect with people.

Because that would be fake.

(continued on page 172)

(continued from page 171)

Never. Gonna. Happen.

Instead of the silly ICA exercises, we need to be doing the work that really mattes.

The ICA work that matters is taking the time to understand the frustrations that your potential fans have related to your area of expertise.

In this week's episode of The Online Genius Podcast, I walk through how to do the ICA work the RIGHT way.

When you do this work the RIGHT way, you can get into your fans' minds and know the conversations they're having with themselves.

Imagine if you knew exactly what your fans and potential customers wanted.

Or if your fans were constantly struck that you seem to know them better than they know themselves.

When you do your ICA work right… that's exactly what happens.

So if you're ready to burrow into your fans brains (in a good way), check out Episode 88 of The Online Genius Podcast.

Talk later.

Bobby

P.S. Because I practice what I preach, I'm constantly trying to better understand my fans. ***I need your advice to help me shape*** the trainings I'm creating to help entrepreneurs like you find, attract, nurture, and serve their TRUE fans. If you haven't yet, do me a favor and click here to give me your advice. I promise not to burrow too far into your head. 😆 🤣

Fundamentally, what most people get wrong is thinking that they should figure out their audience's favorite reality TV show so they can talk about it on their platform. That's dumb advice. You should take a cue from reality TV and create content that lets people into your life so they'll be hooked and will have to keep coming back.[77]

TWO SIMPLE RULES FOR WEEKLY EMAILS

There are two simple rules to keep in mind when writing your weekly emails. Seriously, just two of them, and they are most definitely simple.

Rule number one is kinda a gimme: email your subscriber list each and every week. I mean, it's right there in the name ("weekly" emails). This is about staying top of mind, about connecting, and about your subscribers remembering who you are. They need regular emails so that you become part of their lives. Just like they expect their favorite TV show to air each week, they should grow to expect to hear from you every week. When they come to expect it and know it's coming, it becomes a little treat for them. Each week, they're going to get that email from you and get that reward of an emotional response, whether that's a laugh or a moment of inspiration or delight—whatever your tone evokes.

A lot of entrepreneurs worry that emailing every week will annoy their list. When I hear people express this worry, I

---

77. Now does that mean you have to tell your subscribers everything about your life and let them see every intimate detail? Absolutely not, because real life isn't reality TV. You get to choose what to share and what your boundaries are.

can't help but think, "If sending *one* email a week is going to annoy your people, how the hell are you ever going to sell to them with email?" As you'll learn in the next chapter, when it's time to sell, you'll be sending emails way more frequently than once a week.

But then I think of the second rule: write good emails.[78]

I wanted to leave it at that, but that stick-in-the-mud editor informs me that people might want me to explain *how* to write good emails. Sheesh! You readers are so demanding. Fine. The rest of the chapter will be about how to go about writing good weekly emails.

TELL STORIES, DON'T TALK CONTENT

The first thing you need to do to write good weekly emails is forget everything that other people have taught you about how to write those regular emails. Most people will teach you to focus on your content in the weekly emails. That is a mistake.

While your weekly email will contain *some* content, the core of your weekly email should be a story about you so that you can let your subscribers in on your life.

Your weekly emails should follow the same structure laid out in Chapter 5: hook, story, call to action. (And again, write them backward!)

If you're creating long-form weekly content, like a blog, podcast, or video, the call to action is a very short and sweet summary

---

78. Actually, I tend to think something more like "stop writing shitty emails." But my team has insisted that I be nice rather than being an ass (at least in the body of the book!).

of the content: typically three paragraphs that are one to two sentences each, with a link to the call to action at the beginning and at the end.

If you're not creating regular content, the structure will be modified slightly: hook, story, *lesson*, call to action. The lesson is a very truncated version of what you might say in a blog post, video, or podcast. You're giving some kind of content that can fill the void for now.

The lesson should be something about what you teach. In my case, it would be about entrepreneurship. If you're a fitness person, it'll be about fitness. Then you'll tell the story that relates to that lesson, but the lesson will be more directly about how you serve your people. Think of it as a little tidbit or snippet you want to get across to them. You don't want to make your emails as long as novels, but you do want to be delivering value that they can implement.

The call to action here will relate to whatever the lesson is. It could be to implement what you've just taught them. It could be to hit reply and tell you something or post on social media and tag you. It can be any number of things; you just want to tell them to do *something*.

Remember that you are training your people to expect that your emails are always going to tell them to do something. When you start selling, you're going to tell them to do something, so this is practice. You want them to get used to seeing it so that when you tell them to go sign up for a webinar or buy your product, they don't think, "What?! How *dare* you tell me to do something??" You want their response to be "Yup, of course Bobby is telling me to do something. He orders me around every single email!"

No matter what, the story about your life should be the center of the email. That is the main event. That's what will keep people coming back.

In thinking about what story to use, generally look for personal vignettes, like *Seinfeld*, not epic stories like *Game of Thrones*. If *Seinfeld* could create an entire episode that takes place while the characters are waiting for a table at a Chinese restaurant, imagine what you can do with those little moments from your life.

Every once in a while you can tell an epic story, but typically your stories will be smaller tidbits from your life, not some huge, sweeping adventure that takes forever to tell.

LESSONS FROM TELEVISION

Let's go back to where we started this chapter, to really dial in how to tell a good story in your email. TV writers are masters at telling interesting stories, so we might as well learn from them.

The Role You Play

One thing you pick up on pretty quickly watching TV is that every character eventually falls into a predictable part or role, even as the story changes. That predictability makes people feel comfortable. If possible, you want to find a predictable role that you will play in most of the stories you tell.

My emails cast me in familiar roles. I'm nearly always the butt of the joke. In fact, you could probably capture about 95 percent of the stories I tell as "dumb stuff Bobby's done." Similarly, I cast myself as someone who *seems* to be randomly lucking into finding the right answers as an entrepreneur. Put another way, I cast myself very much as the entrepreneur equivalent of Detective Columbo from the old TV show. Although any individual email might seem like luck, my habit of lucking into things sends the message that I'm not actually as bumbling as it might seem.[79]

Now, before you go running off to cast yourself as Detective Columbo, I'm not telling you *what* role to pick for yourself. Maybe you're the jokester rather than the butt of the jokes. Maybe you're a Rachel, a Ross, or a Phoebe. The point is simply to be consistent, to create a sense of continuity and familiarity. People see you in that role, and they feel at home reading your emails.

Include Recurring Guest Stars

Another useful technique is to include other people from your life in recurring roles in your emails. My readers have learned to expect my wife and team members to serve as the voice of reason to my wacky persona. People have gotten to know my wife as the person who rolls her eyes at me frequently because I miss something or do something dumb. And they have learned to feel sorry for Katie (my number two) because she is constantly putting up with my antics.

What's funny is that my readers actually feel for the other people in my stories more than for me. They're like, "Oh my goodness, these poor people have to put up with Bobby and his craziness!"

---

79. Hey, I might actually know what I'm doing! I hope that's not too much of a surprise for you, three-quarters of the way through this book you paid for.

And that's intentional. I use those examples with my family or team on purpose, so my readers can have empathy with that person who has to put up with me in my screwball role.

They Shall Go Nameless

I don't ever use my wife's or daughter's names in my emails. I just refer to them as my wife and daughter. That's a personal choice. My wife has asked that I don't post pictures of her or our daughter on social media or in my emails, so I don't.

You can draw the line wherever you're comfortable. And despite the fact that I don't speak in detail about the two people closest to me in my life, I have still built a connection and a friendship with the people on my list. It is absolutely possible to do so without having to share every last bit of your life.

Include Recurring Themes

Another advanced technique you can use is having themes based around things you like or hobbies you do on a regular basis. If you're telling stories from your life, this should tend to happen naturally. Things you do frequently will obviously come up pretty regularly. For me, one of those things is beer because I used to brew beer and almost started a brewery. That's something people have come to know about me, and it's an area that lets them connect with me.

But you could certainly be more intentional about picking themes. Think through things you care about to create an ongoing theme, whether it's hobbies, likes, or other interests. If you focus on things you do on a regular basis, you won't have a super-hard time coming up with ideas of what to write about.

A quick warning: these themes should be relatable to a large portion of your people because the goal is still to create connection. You're looking for common ground and for stories that will have your subscribers thinking, "I've had the same thing happen to me." That means you don't want to talk about things that are completely foreign to your audience.

This doesn't mean that if you have a very specific hobby that isn't relatable to the general public you can *never* talk about it. You can mention it every once in a while—it's still something that allows them to get to know you. But if it's something that your people won't understand or relate to, don't focus heavily on it.

Finally, you can create inside jokes, callbacks, and Easter eggs, just like you see if you watch sitcoms on TV. Kind of like how every *Seinfeld* episode supposedly has a reference to or Easter egg about Superman, and *Psych* has a pineapple hidden in nearly every episode. When you create these inside jokes, the people who have been on your list for a while feel special. It's like they're insiders who are getting that extra level.

A WORD ABOUT NEWSLETTERS

For a long time, I treated the word "newsletter" as a curse word. Newsletter seemed to be code for an email that collected and regurgitated *a lot* of content. 'Cause if rehashing one piece of content is good…talking about lots of content must be better, right?

But it turns out they can have a place. If you are a prolific content creator, you definitely want to tell your audience about all the content you're creating. That's where a newsletter can come into play. But a newsletter should be *in addition to*, not in lieu of, a story-based weekly email.

And for the love of all that is holy, don't make your newsletter boring! I mean, you should try to make sure that *nothing* you create is boring, but this is especially true of your emails. If the choice is between a boring newsletter or not sending one… don't send one. Your newsletter should help connect with your audience by letting your personality shine through.

We recently added a newsletter to our weekly routine, and people have loved it. Not because it's a newsletter, but because it's not your typical newsletter. Here's an example:

From: Bobby Klinck

Date: June 25, 2021

Subject: "Is that what you're wearing?!?!"

(continued on page 181)

(continued from page 180)

Your weekly dose of snark and marketing wisdom

From the desk of Bobby Klinck

After my shower this morning I threw on my Social Media Marketing World t-shirt that I got back in 2019.

When my wife saw me, she said with a shocked tone:

"Is that what you're wearing?!?"

From her response, you'd think she was worried about how I was dressing for a date night.

Nope.

She was worried about how I was going to show up for Day 1 of a bootcamp we're running for my group coaching program this weekend.

She thought I would dress up. Finally, it was my turn to roll my eyes at her (instead of the way more common reverse situation!!!).

And that brings me to this week's rant…

(continued on page 182)

(continued from page 181)

Weekly Rant

One of my biggest pet peeves is marketing advice that's about hiding the real you.

Now, people rarely phrase it that way, but a lot of what we are being told to do is about putting on an outward facing image that isn't the real us.

Take social media photo shoots as an example.

I always laugh when I am scrolling social media and see the clearly staged photos that are meant to look like people are just doing ordinary things.

The funniest example for me is when I see people who are dressed to the nines with perfectly coiffed hair reading a marketing book.

But here's my question:

Who the hell dresses up to read a book????

More likely, you're reading that book in workout clothes or pajamas with bedhead.

(At least that's how you'll find ME reading books).

What's with the obsession with pretending to be something we aren't to please other people's crazy idea of what we should be doing?

That brings me to the tip…

Marketing Tip

My marketing tip for you is simple… be authentically you. It makes business way more fun (and it's good for your business too!).

One of my coaching members was complaining at one point about how showing up on social media was exhausting for her.

(continued on page 183)

(continued from page 182)

When we dug into it, everything made sense. She was spending her time showing up how she thought she was supposed to show up.

Social media had become a chore because it meant putting on a different face (but with a smile!!!).

Yeah. Screw that noise.

If you are spending your time being anything but your authentic self, it will exhaust you.

And you'll give up, which is bad for business.

So instead of picking some social media approach because someone says it's what you're supposed to be doing, maybe try just being yourself.

(Assuming, of course, that you're not a total arsehole.)

If you wear beat up Social Media Marketing World t-shirts in your everyday life… feel free to wear them when you show up to a bootcamp or on social media!

Try it… you just might like it.

And your real fans will thank you for being you.

Recommended Resource

This week's recommended resource is a no-brainer… it's our newest course inside BOMU — BADA$$ List Building.

I'm not one to say that any one form of marketing is best, but you'd be hard pressed to find one that's more effective than email marketing.

And it all starts with getting people to sign up for your list!

(continued on page 184)

(continued from page 183)

If you've been paying attention to the podcast the past few weeks, we've been talking list building.

BADA$$ List Building takes it to the next level with a full course to teach you how to grow a list that will power your business.

And you can get it absolutely free inside BOMU!

If you aren't a BOMU student yet, click here to grab your spot!

Special Promo

When we first launched Smart-Ass Marketing, I told you that this would be the exclusive place to get discounts going forward.

Today is the first time that's coming into play!

My team and I wanted to come up with a way to help people implement the information inside the new BADA$$ List Building course.

So we'll be running a List Building Bootcamp on July 15 and 16, to help people get shit done.

Bootcamps are going to become a regular staple of our business because we love the idea of helping people move at the speed of Bobby (aka get shit done in days, not weeks or months).

During the List Building Bootcamp, we'll be helping people go from idea to built opt-in funnel in a matter of 2 days.

You'll walk away with a brand new lead magnet, a high-converting opt-in page, your delivery email, and a FB Ad to drive traffic to the freebie.

This will be a relatively small event where people will get the chance to work hand-in-hand with me, my team, and BOM certified coaches.

Click Here To Check Out The Details

(continued on page 185)

(continued from page 184)

Now for that discount I teased… You can get $100 off the bootcamp by using coupon code "EARLYBIRD" when you checkout (without the quotation marks!).

If you need help getting your list building into gear, we'd love to see you at the bootcamp. (Just don't expect me to dress up for it!)

Content Roundup

Here's a quick recap of the content you might have missed this week:

BLOG POST: CAN YOU REALLY START AN ONLINE BUSINESS WITH NO MONEY DOWN? - Real talk… can you start a business with no money down? Check out my answer in this post and let me know what you think.

BLOG POST: 5 MUST-HAVE EMAIL SEQUENCES FOR ONLINE ENTREPRENEURS - If you have a knowledge based online business, there are 5 types of email sequences that you need. Check out this post and let me know how many of these you already have.

BLOG POST: WHY THE ONLINE MARKETING MODEL IS BROKEN - Ever feel frustrated by some of the practices in the online marketing industry? In this post, I'm sharing some of the issues I keep seeing and would be interested to hear your concerns and ideas for moving forward.

VIDEO: How To Never Run Out Of Content Ideas | Bobby Ruins Marketing - So many entrepreneurs focus their time and effort on creating social media even though it will disappear and spend little or no time creating lasting content that is truly evergreen. In this video, I offer a better approach.

VIDEO: How To Build Your Email List With Great Stories | Bobby Ruins Marketing Email Edition - What if people opened your emails no matter what the subject line said? That's the difference that good stories can make in your email. Check out this video to learn how to add awesome stories to your email marketing.

(continued on page 186)

(continued from page 185)

PODCAST: THE INBOUND JOURNEY: CREATING A HIGH-CONVERTING OPT-IN PAGE - Today we're getting into the weeds of list building. We'll be breaking down how to build a high-converting opt-in page so that people will want to join your list.

That's all for this week... now off to run that bootcamp for my coaching people.

What makes Smart-Ass Marketing work is that it's uniquely me. There are tidbits of stories, including recurring characters, and my voice and tone come through in spades. The "content recap" is almost an afterthought.

If you're going to create a newsletter, infuse it with your personality. And if you do it right, you might just get an email response like this:

> I know Team BOM gets tons of emails, but I can't resist providing feedback any longer. THANK YOU for these new weekly emails and your frank insights on the online business world, Bobby. I didn't realize how much I wanted more Bobby until you started delivering MORE BOBBY to my inbox. Many thanks for what you do in your corner of the online business world.

That's right, one of my subscribers literally thanked me for emailing her *more* often. Because she felt a connection to me, she loved hearing from me a second time each week.

GIVE 'EM A GLIMPSE

You have to crawl before you walk and then run. Don't feel like you have to have a well-crafted plan for your persona, themes, and recurring characters when you first start.

Just start by telling stories. That one shift will make your weekly emails better than 95 percent of the ones that hit people's inboxes. As you get good at it, you'll start to find your rhythm. Then, once you feel like you're in a comfortable rhythm, start thinking about what roles you play or what topics you can bring back.

These themes are jokes in my emails, but they also are part of my social media presence. Part of my bigger content piece is me playing those roles. Don't try to force it to apply where it doesn't. But where it actually works, you're entertaining your audience so they get to know and like you even more.

When people have been reading my emails and then meet me, they're not going to feel like I'm somebody different. They'll feel like they know me even better because they've read my emails and already had those weekly glimpses into my life. (Reading my emails feels like coming home. Awww.)

There's one more thing weekly emails do, and it's likely what you've been looking for since the beginning of this book: your weekly emails will also start priming your readers to buy. In the next chapter, we'll tackle how to sell stuff.

CHAPTER 10

STEP FIVE: SELL SOME STUFF WITH A SALES SEQUENCE

REMEMBER WAY BACK IN THE BEGINNING OF THIS BOOK when I quoted Peter Drucker's views on marketing versus selling? Just in case you missed it or your brain is full of all the other email marketing you've learned since then, I'll include it again here:

> There will always, one can assume, be a need for some selling. But the aim of marketing is to make selling superfluous. The aim of marketing is to know and understand the customer so well that the product or service fits him and sells itself. Ideally, marketing should result in a

customer who is ready to buy. All that should be needed then is to make the product or service available.[80]

And I made it sound as if he was infallible. Well, I played a bit of a trick on you. Sorry. With all due respect, Peter Drucker was wrong, kind of.

As much as we would all love that to be true—an ideal world where you don't have to sell, where people line up to throw money at you[81]—it just isn't reality. Some people are going to say, "Yes, I want it!" as soon as you send that first email, but most people aren't.

For the majority of your list, the reality is that in order to get people to buy...you're going to have to sell.

You're going to have to do some persuading. That's where a well-written sales sequence comes in.

THE GOAL: DELIVER THE RIGHT CONVERSION MESSAGES

Are you ready to learn how to sell some stuff with email?! Who am I kidding? That's almost certainly why you bought the book in the first place—you are a marketer, after all.

I've got some good news for you: if you've followed along to this point, you are well on your way to effortless email selling. By taking people on a journey, you have moved them from cold leads to warm followers (and maybe even raving fans). You

---

80. You want that footnote again? Okay, here you go: Peter Drucker, *Management: Tasks, Responsibilities, Practices* (New York: Harper and Row, 1973), 64–65.

81. That's probably not exactly what Peter Drucker meant…but, man, it's nice to dream!

should have a lot of people who are ready to buy. Some will be willing to buy right away, based on little more than you making an offer (like Drucker said). But most of your people will still need a little nudge in the right direction. Selling to those people is about creating a high-converting sales sequence.

Before you object that you *hate* selling, don't worry: this sales sequence isn't set up to make you feel dirty or sleazy. An effective sales sequence isn't about dirty tricks; it's about hitting the right selling points that different buyer types need in order to make their decision to buy from you. The rub is that it isn't just a matter of sending some emails with random conversion copy elements to them. Nope, there's some psychology to it all.

Simply? This chapter is all about how to write the right emails, in the right order, to actually get your audience to buy.

Bobby's Swift Kick in the Ass

One of the big mistakes I see entrepreneurs make is assuming that everyone thinks like them. They object to writing a full sales page or creating long sales emails because *they* never read long sales copy.

Newsflash: not everyone thinks like you. There are impulsive buyers (like me) who tend to be presold. Those kinds of buyers don't need all the details and don't really care about emotional stories. But there are also detail buyers who need to know *all* the information. And there are emotional buyers who need to connect with stories of other people.

Anytime you are creating sales copy, you have to recognize that you are speaking to people who approach purchases from very different frames of mind. That means doing your best to speak to all the potential buyers.

Everything else in the book has been leading up to this, but we're also going to be departing from a lot of the things you've already read. Let me be very clear, though, particularly if you just skipped to this chapter and haven't read Chapters 1 through 9: *everything else is necessary in order for this to really work*. If people don't know who the heck you are and feel no connection to you, selling is going to be really freaking hard.

The point of being in business is to make money, so this is the culmination of all your other efforts. It is *not* the shortcut to skipping ahead. If you haven't done the other pieces, guess what? The most beautiful sales sequence written by the best copywriter won't do you much good if you haven't built a connection with your audience before you go to sell. On the other hand, a decent sales sequence you write yourself will work just fine if you have done all the other stuff in this book.

At the same time, you can't just wimp out and decide not to do this because you think it's hard. Let me be clear: *it is hard*. Sales emails are the hardest emails you're going to have to write, because you have to be tactical and strategic. It's not just about telling stories; it's about thinking through everything your audience needs and wants, and how they think about where they are and where they want to be.

The reason this works so well is because you've built the connection, so your audience is open to listening to you. They know, like, and trust you. So you have to be willing to do it. The good news is that if you've written a sales page[82] that hits a lot of these points, you'll be able to pull out some of the concepts and content from that sales page and use it here.

Everything you've been doing with your email marketing has all been leading to this point. It's time to make some money. So strap in—this is everything you need and want to know, and it's gonna be a long one!

SIX CORE EMAILS

The sales sequence is a very specific, intentional series of emails sent out in deliberate order to take people on a sales journey (and to speak to different buyer types at different times). While there are countless emails that you could send, there are six types of emails that should be included in just about every sales sequence. Here they are in the order you should send them:

Value Load

The first email you send is what I call the *value load* email. Like the name suggests, it is about loading up the value so your potential buyers immediately recognize that your offer is an amazeballs deal. This email lays out the offer in detail, including the benefits of buying and the features of your product. Having finished reading this email, people should understand exactly

---

82. You *have* written a sales page, haven't you? (The answer should be yes!)

what they will get, what it will cost them, and how their life will be different if they buy.

This will generally be one of the longest emails you'll send during your promotional sequence because there is a lot of ground to cover. It takes a lot of words to lay out the benefits and features. With that in mind, I recommend keeping the story at the top short and to-the-point on this one. In fact, an analogy often works better than a story here.

When I was launching the all-access pass to my legal template library, I often used an analogy to a Chinese food buffet. Here's one version I sent:

I've just opened the doors to my signature legal template offering, The Online Genius Template Library.

… but before we talk about that, we need to talk about Chinese food.

I love so many different kinds of Chinese food: Kung pao chicken… General Tso's chicken… Mongolian beef… sweet and sour pork… double cooked pork… pepper steak with onions… and I could go on!

I can't do a la carte Chinese anymore. I don't want one thing.

But a buffet… a glorious buffet lets me get ALL the things.

And it's not about quantity. The beauty of the buffet is the variety.

The Online Genius Template Library *is kind of like a Chinese food buffet but for your "legal stuff."*

The goal of this analogy is simply to give people a quick anchor to understand the offer (and to answer the question of why to get the all-access pass rather than individual templates). The value load email uses a short one- or two-paragraph analogy rather than a detailed, in-depth story because you want to get straight to the point.

You are trying to do three major things with this email:

- First, you're giving your subscribers the CliffsNotes version of your offer. After reading it, they should know exactly what they're going to get, what it's going to cost, and what the process is. In many ways, it's the condensed version of a sales page for your product.

- Second, this email highlights the benefits people will get from buying your product. If they do the work, how will their life be transformed? It can't simply be about the deliverables they get. You have to tell them why it matters and how they'll be in a better position because they take you up on this offer. This is the central value proposition of your offer.

- Finally, you need to talk about the essential features. In writing conversion copy, we often hear that we shouldn't fixate on features, that we should talk about the benefits instead. That's true, but people still want to know what they're going to get. This is where, if you're selling an online course, for example, you can lay out how many modules are in the course, what each module is, and what they're going to learn in each.

Those are the three required elements. If you have limited-time bonuses, you will also highlight those in this email, especially if you have a first-day bonus that is designed to create urgency. Use this email to get subscribers excited and wanting to buy.

You have to make the offer to people, but your first email will obviously tend to speak most directly to people who are impulsive and spontaneous buyers (like me!). Giving them a reason to buy right away just makes the decision even easier for them, which is why limited-time bonuses work so well at the beginning of a promotion. If you have limited-time bonuses, mentioning them here will motivate those spontaneous buyers to act right away. You're also starting to hit the details for the detail people, but no matter what kind of buyer they are, people want to know what they're going to get.

So that you can get the full effect, here is an entire value load email that I sent during one promotion of my template library. Rather than the Chinese food analogy, I used value anchoring:

From: Bobby Klinck

Subject: Protect your business without sending me on a European vacation

Hey Jillian,

I've just opened the doors to <u>The Online Genius Template Library</u>— the A-Z legal template library to help online entrepreneurs protect their businesses.

(continued on page 197)

(continued from page 196)

But before we talk about that, I want to tell you about the **stupidest business decision I ever made**.

(Whoops! I broke the rules right away... I mean, how many marketers would tell you about doing something stupid right out of the gate!)

So what was the monumentally stupid decision?

I hired a coach to help me develop a "high-ticket" offer.

I'm not against high-ticket offers... I love working with coaches... and I have nothing against the coach I hired...

...so, why was it a stupid decision, then?

Well, as a lawyer, I don't exactly need help crafting a high-ticket offer... *high-ticket is kind of the default setting for lawyers.*

You want me to customize one of my templates for your business... that'll be $1,500. 💲

You want me to create a single bespoke contract for you... I'll gladly do it for $5,000! 💲 💲

You want me to set you up with customized agreements for all your legal needs... now we're talking a European vacation for my family! 💲 ✈️ 💲

For a lawyer, the hard part isn't creating a high-ticket offer...

...the challenge is creating *legal solutions that aren't high-ticket.* You know, the kind that are affordable if you don't have five grand in pocket change!

That's where The Online Genius Template Library comes in.

(continued on page 198)

(continued from page 197)

When you grab the Template Library, you get ALL OF THE TEMPLATES to protect your business, including:

- **Website Legal Policies** - The 3 templates you MUST have on your website if you want your butt to be 100% covered.

- **Customer/Client Agreements** - Go-to contracts for anyone who books one-to-one services with you.

- **Online Program Terms and Conditions** - Agreements for your online courses and membership sites with all the legalese included, including the oh-so-important refund policy!

- **Confidentiality Agreements** - Templates to help you protect the "secret sauce" in your business.

- **Independent Contractor Agreement** - Make sure your relationship with your VA, copywriter, designer, and other outside contractors doesn't create risks for your business.

- **Agreements for Employees** - The must-have contracts to ensure you own the content they create for you and that they don't walk out the door with your confidential information.

- **Publicity, Testimonial, and Podcast Releases** - The ritten consent you NEED for anyone who appears on your online platform.

- **Affiliate Agreement** - Having people sell your product FOR you is a dream… as long as you've got a written agreement with your affiliates to make sure you don't end up in a nasty dispute.

- **LLC Operating Agreement** - The basic agreement you NEED to protect yourself and your business.

You'll be getting ALL OF THE THINGS!

(continued on page 199)

(continued from page 198)

This is the legal toolbox that will serve you now and in the future. As your business grows, you'll ***already*** have the agreements and templates you'll need.

*Imagine how soundly you'll sleep once you've got all the right agreements in place… **knowing the legal stuff is under control**.*

When you sign up for The Online Genius Template Library, you'll also get access to a private Facebook group that's only for my students. I'll be there to answer your questions about the templates and about the "legal stuff" more generally.

But wait… there's more! (One day, I really want to say that out loud!!! 🤣😆)

As I add legal templates to my online store… they'll be added to the Template Library. That's right… if I decide to create a Speaker Agreement Template or a Mastermind Agreement Template, you'll get those too!

Like I said… you'll get ALL OF THE THINGS to protect your business.

The best part?

You don't have to send my family to Europe to grab the Library. Heck, you don't even have to pay what it'd cost to get me to create one agreement for you.

Nope. For just $997 (or monthly payments of $97), you can get ALL THE LEGAL TEMPLATES!

Look, if you've got more money than time, give me a call 📞. We can chat about you sending me on that European vacation…

…otherwise, why don't you just take me up on this limited-time offer to get all the legal templates you need without breaking the bank.

(continued on page 200)

(continued from page 199)

Talk later.

Bobby

FAST ACTION BONUS

I've got a SPECIAL bonus for people who take action today!

I love action takers and I love getting to talk with amazing entrepreneurs, so I've decided to throw in an extra special bonus for anyone who buys today.

A 30-minute one-on-one call with me to create a legal roadmap (or to chat about anything else you'd like to talk about).

This bonus has a lot of entrepreneurs in my mastermind group mimicking my favorite line from *Top Gun*...

"*You're gonna do whatttttt?*"

They all seem to think my time is too valuable to give 30 minutes to all the action-takers...

...I say screw 'em.

I'm here to help you get peace of mind, and the quickest way for me to have you chillin like a Buddhist monk is to jump on the phone one-on-one with you.

To claim this fast action bonus, you've got to grab the Template Library before midnight tonight!

P.S. I'm going to be sending some additional emails about the Template Library launch over the coming days. If you love my emails generally (I mean, who doesn't?!?!) but would rather not hear about the Template Library any more, just click here and I won't send you emails about this promotion.

Cost of Inaction

After you've laid out the offer with a value load email, the next type of email to send is one that details the *cost of inaction*. People need to understand how not acting is hurting them. The reality is that people won't buy until they recognize that the cost of not acting is greater than the cost of acting.

This email is about what copywriters call agitating the pain. But this is not about being an ass and making people feel like crap just for the hell of it. It's not about fearmongering or coming up with a fake, bullshit pain point or a parade of horribles that are unlikely to come to pass.[83] That is *not* what this is about.

This is about making sure people recognize what can happen and where they are—and what will continue to happen if they don't act. The approach you'll take to this email depends on whether your offer is about solving an existing pain point or is a prophylactic solution.

If your product solves a *current* pain or frustration, this email is about making sure people recognize that they are actually in pain. The pain may have even become their new normal, living in this world of "that's just how life is." So even if they're not conscious of being in a constant state of pain or frustration, you have to help them see it. They're probably not going to buy a product that solves a problem if they don't think they have that problem.

For this type of email, you don't have to frame it as what will happen if they don't buy your product; you can simply talk about

---

83. You can tell I get worked up about people who use these tactics because the curse words start flying!

their current pain and how your offer solves it. By pointing out their current pain and offering your product as a solution, you are helping them to see their current pain and the cost of not acting.

If your product is about avoiding *future* pain, you have to do something a bit different. In that case, you will create something akin to a negative case study. In other words, you tell people the story of someone who didn't act and had a bad result. This is the approach I took with my legal templates, telling the story of a friend who had to give a $4,500 refund to someone who didn't deserve it because she had "gapped" it and didn't get her agreements in place. The story helped people see that the risks I talk about are *real*, not imagined.

If you don't have a specific real-life example like that, don't make one up. That's not cool. Instead, write a story that helps people understand and feel that pain. For example, if you're a health and wellness coach, maybe you want to tell people the cost of being prediabetic and talk about what that actually does in the body.

With this email, you are transitioning to the emotional, social-proof buyers. Citing a bunch of statistics likely isn't the best way to go—but if that's all you've got, make it work. The more you can tell it in a story form, the better, because stories and emotions resonate with people more than facts and figures.

Case Study

Next up is your *case study* email. A quick note: even if you add some of the optional emails that we'll talk about later in the chapter, make sure the case study comes right after the cost of inaction email. This order is important because you are imme-diately contrasting the pain they are in (or could be in) with the good results that are possible.

Case studies are simply testimonials told in story form. Choose one of your success stories—ideally for the product you're selling. If you don't have that, step back and talk about someone that you've helped one-on-one. If you're selling a course, talk about someone you've helped for free. Use that story to sell this same service, in the context of where that person was before and how they were struggling.

Because this email comes right after the cost of inaction email, you can tie in that this person was in the same pain you described there. But then they worked with you or bought your product, and that solved their problem.

Describe the hell they were in, in such a way that your audi-ence will feel like they are there too. Of course, they *don't want to be there*. Use words that will resonate with them. Tell about how purchasing your product was the catalyst for change that transformed that person's painful situation. This is how their life will also be better as a result. (This is very similar to the transfor-mation you talked about in your value load email. Are you seeing how this entire journey is woven together to form one piece?)

You can't assume that people have read the earlier emails, so don't skip talking about the pain point in this email. Spend time making the pain point clear—the frustration and the struggle in the context of where they are. This may be as simple as they weren't where they wanted to be before they started working with you, and then you gave them a jump start.

A Legal Note about Case Studies

Believe it or not, the way that nearly every online marketing teacher, coach, and guru is teaching you to use testimonials and case studies is illegal. The typical advice is to collect "results-based" testimonials (e.g., "I followed Bobby's advice and made $857 million"[84]) and present those with a small disclaimer on the bottom of the page that says something like "results aren't typical." Does that sound about like what you've been told to do?

People teaching you to do that are telling you to *break the law*. No, seriously. That advice isn't just shady because it gives people false hope. It is illegal, plain and simple.

Under the Federal Trade Commission (FTC) rules, you are not allowed to present the results from your most successful students as case studies unless you also disclose what the typical results are. Yeah, you read that right. A "results not typical" disclaimer is not enough. You have to actually tell people what the typical results are.

About now, you probably want to protest, "But Bobby, I don't have data about what the typical results are!" My only response is "too bad." If you want to make claims about results (whether directly or by presenting results-based case studies), you have the obligation to collect the data to support claims about typical results. If you don't have that data, you cannot make claims.

If you don't have data to support results claims, your case studies and testimonials should relate to things other than results. Things like ease of use, the support the people writing the testimonials

---

84. To be clear, no one has ever said that about me, and I make no promises that you will make $857 million or any other amount of money by using what I teach.

received, and how they feel. These testimonials aren't as effective from a sales perspective, but at least you won't be breaking the law.

There are some special cases. If you have a very well-known person in your space who uses your product, you might not need a case study. You can simply point out that this person has chosen to use your product. That gives credibility where you're almost saying, "You can use the exact same product as Well-Known Person, and you can be like that person!" Be sure to get permission from that person before you use their name, but if you do, you can do that without having to tell it as a story.

Only use one case study per email (so choose the best one). You'll see later in this chapter where you can include additional emails with more testimonials.

Solicit Questions

The fourth must-send email is one simply to *solicit questions*. The gist is pretty simple: "I would hate for you not to buy because there's some question in your mind that I haven't answered. If you're thinking you might be interested and you have a question, hit reply and tell me about it, and I'll answer your question."

Asking people to reply to your email is the simplest way to go, but you can do something more advanced. There are multiple apps for your smartphone that will let you grab a new text-messaging number. With one of these apps, you can literally tell people to "text" you rather than email. This blows people away because they are not used to that level of access to the people who are marketing to them.

This may seem like something that will take a ton of your time, but it is worth it! When I have these kinds of conversations, 80 percent of those people have ended up buying. You might not convert 80 percent right away, but you should be converting well over 50 percent of the people who do engage, so it's worth doing. (If it's not worth it to you, we should probably have a different discussion right now. How'd you even make it this far?)

Not everyone is going to take you up on this, but if you go with this approach, your very willingness to give that level of access will convince some people to buy.[85] That's why the email soliciting questions is a staple of every promo I run.

Frequently Asked Questions

Next up is a *frequently asked questions* email. This will likely be the longest email you'll send because you'll be answering a ton of questions. Your FAQ email is about addressing objections, but you word them as questions. By answering those questions, you help people make the right decision about whether to buy.

You know your audience and your offer better than I do, but here are three questions I think every FAQ should have:

- **"What do I get again?"** Answering that question allows you to recap the offer.

---

85. True story: the first time I sent the "text me" email, someone responded saying something like "I don't have any questions, but just the fact that you are willing to do this got me off the fence. I'm in!" In my most recent promotion, our analytics showed this email resulted in more sales than any other…and *no one* even texted me.

- **"Who is this program for?"** Then you can recap who it's designed for.

- **"Who is this program *not* for?"** As strange as it seems, answering this one can be a big help in getting people to buy. Explaining who the program is not for will help people who are a good fit see that it will work for them. In a sense, seeing all the people it's *not* for helps the people it *is for* see that it's right for them.

Beyond that, your FAQs should address objections or obstacles that buyers are likely to have. You've probably already addressed a lot of these in the FAQ section on your sales page, so you can pull from that. You don't have to reinvent the wheel.

Put the questions in bold so people can scan through and see the question they want, then read the response. Not everybody is going to read everything. Keep the formatting simple, and make it easy for them to find the information they need.

You should know in advance what most of these questions will be and have them pretty well written out, but feel free to add questions as the promotion proceeds (and before you send this email out). If you are getting questions you didn't anticipate, definitely include them in this email.

Urgency Emails

For a promotion to work well, you generally need to provide some *urgency*—a reason why people should buy now. It could be that you have bonuses expiring or that the cart will close and the product won't be available for a certain period.

Assuming you have some form of urgency, you should have one or more emails on the last day that highlight the urgency to buy now. The number of urgency emails you send should be proportional to the urgency at stake. If it's just a bonus that is going away, sending a single stand-alone urgency email might be enough. If you are closing cart and your program won't be available for a whole year, you should send 857 urgency emails. Okay, that might be a bit of an exaggeration, but it is normal to send three to five emails on cart-close day.[86] Every single one of them should highlight the urgency.

If you are sending multiple cart-close emails, you'll want to find different themes for different emails. For a midday email, you might tell a story about how you forgot to do something really important because you put it off until the last minute. Something like this:

From: Bobby Klinck

Subject: Don't screw up like I did.

I really *screwed* up recently.

One night around 8:30 PM, I was working like mad on a promo, when my dad called.

(continued on page 209)

---

86. If you think sending that many emails to your list will lead to a mutiny, don't worry. I've got a simple solution we'll talk about in a bit.

(continued from page 208)

It seemed like silly chit-chat, so I was multitasking (talking to him while tweaking an email).

Then I heard my brother in the background, which was weird for a random Monday.

Then I thought about it… and looked at the date on my watch.

Shit!!!

It was my Dad's birthday (his 75th no less!), and I had forgotten to call him.

The kicker is that I'd specifically thought about it earlier that day. When I was dropping my daughter off at school, I mentioned that we needed to call "Pops" to wish him a happy birthday after school…

…but then I got busy ***and forgot***.

(See where I'm going with this?)

This email isn't about me, Jillian.

I'm sending it because you haven't pulled the trigger on <u>The Online Genius Template Library yet</u>.

I know you're a smarty pants… I mean, you signed up for the free training because you KNEW you needed to get your legal stuff in place, right?

…so I'm guessing you haven't clicked buy yet because you've been busy.

Well, I'd hate for you to screw up like I did!

Your chance to grab The Online Genius Template Library ends tonight!

You could put it on your list of things to do later today… but then you might forget.

(continued on page 210)

(continued from page 209)

So how about we don't do that, okay?

Let's stop what you're doing right now, <u>head over, and grab your spot right now, okay</u>?

Talk later.

Bobby

P.S. Hopefully, you have all the information you need by now. But if there's a BURNING question you need answered, before you <u>grab all my legal templates</u>, you can reply and ask.

Pretty sure I will never come up with a better "don't wait or you might forget" story than that one!

The final urgency email you send should literally tell your subscribers this is their last chance. The central message is "Last call. This is it. I'm not going to email you anymore. This is your last chance." You can make a reference to last call at a bar or whatever fits your style, but it's simply telling people that this is the last time they'll hear from you about this, and they probably don't want to miss out.

Apparently, I'm good at urgency emails because I used a staple story for my *last* email that became a bit of a legendary email:

From: Bobby Klinck

Subject: Let's avoid the walk of shame, shall we?

My keystone habit is going for a long morning walk or run, so I hit the door around 5 am each day.

And let me tell you this… there are some FUNNY things happening on the streets of Washington, DC at 7 am.

About a month ago, I noticed that I kept seeing people who were dressed like they were heading to "the club."

Women in knee high boots and skirts so short they'd make Daisy Duke blush!

Men in crazy suits and shirts that were a few shades too bright to be worn in the light of day.

I was baffled…

As always, it was my wife to the rescue.

When I mentioned it to her, she looked at me, rolled her eyes, and said:

"Dummy, they're doing the walk of shame."

 D'uh!

But this isn't an email about my mind not going to the gutter… it's about you!

Let's make sure you're not doing a metaphorical walk of shame tomorrow…

Time is running out for you to grab <u>The Online Genius Template Library</u>, so you can get all the legal templates you need.

(continued on page 212)

(continued from page 211)

Doors close at midnight eastern time.

Time may be running out, but the good news is that there's still time to avoid shame.

Even if you've waited til the last minute, you can still dive in and get your business protected in no-time flat.

Take it from Karen who was one of THE LAST people to grab her spot in the Template Library last time I launched it:

Hi Bobby Klinck and members of the group! I must like living on the edge because I purchased your template library 45 minutes before the offer expired, and it was the best decision I've made for my business to date! Legal things I've spent months agonizing over I was able to complete in one afternoon.... Your template library had everything I needed. Thank you.

Like you…she waited until the last minute.

Even though she did the high-wire act… the Template Library was a blessing to her. She said buying what "the best decision" she ever made!

And she got her protection in place in one afternoon.

You're coming down to the wire here, so how about we get you to repeat Karen's story.

Click here to **grab ALL my legal templates** before the pre-sale runs out!

Talk later.

Bobby

(continued on page 213)

(continued from page 212)

P.S. Are you still reading but haven't bought yet?!? Come on, I'm not that funny. My wife tells me just about every day. If you are reading the PS line in my final email in this promotion, you clearly KNOW you need to jump at this opportunity. Here's how to do that. Quit reading already. Go join The Online Genius Template Library.

In case you're wondering, that story is 100 percent true. No exaggeration. Actually happened. And my wife still can't believe I didn't understand what was happening.

Pay special attention to that PS line. The theme in that PS section is something that you should always use in your final email of a promotion. If they are still reading your emails that late in the promotion, they are either copy nerds (like me) or they are interested in what you have to offer. Assume the latter, and point that out to them.

Bobby's Swift Kick in the Ass

For the love of all that is holy, do not tell people you are ending a promotion (whether closing the cart or removing bonuses) and then send a "surprise, I've decided to extend the offer" email. For some reason, a lot of online marketers forget the basic rule that lying is wrong.

Don't lie to people to get them to buy.

> Seriously, if you think that's okay, send this book back to me, and I'll give you a refund. The last thing I want is any of my email marketing wizardry used for nefarious purposes!
>
> If someone reaches out to you after the deadline and begs for an extension, you can make that individual decision, but don't act like you're closing the cart when you know damn well you're not. That's called lying, and lying to people is bad, in email or otherwise.

OTHER EMAILS

While the six types of emails listed above are ones you should include in nearly every promotion, there are others that you might want to use as well, depending on the length of the promotional period. For a promotional period that's ten days or less, you are going to send at least one email a day, so you'll have some slots to fill. Here are some ideas for extra emails you can send during the promotion period.

Bonus Emails

If you include bonuses that expire at certain points during a promotion period, you're going to need to introduce the bonuses and tell people when they're going to expire. This can include one or two stand-alone emails per bonus. For a really dynamite bonus, you'll want to devote an entire email to announcing it. Other bonuses you might announce in a PS line on one of the other emails.

Regardless of how you announce the bonus, you should have an email that reminds people to buy before it expires. These types of emails are similar to the urgency emails set out above, but the focus is on the bonus ending rather than the entire promotion.

Alternative Costs

One of my favorite emails is the alternative cost email. In a weeklong promotional period, this email would typically go out the day after the value load email. It goes out before the cost of inaction or anything else because you're anchoring value. Where the cost of inaction email asks what it costs them to do nothing, the alternative cost email shows people what it would cost to solve the same problem another way. With this email, you are anchoring the value of the solution your product provides to something that is much more expensive.

The value load email I shared had hints of this alternative cost (because I didn't have time to do it as a stand-alone email in that promotion). The email asked, "Do you want to send my family on a European vacation?" I highlighted the point that the cost to hire me to create custom legal agreements would be $5,000 to $10,000. They could do that and send me and my family on a European vacation…or, for $1,000, they could get all my legal templates and do it themselves.

These emails are considerably more effective than the ridiculous way that *most* people try to establish value. For some reason, people have been convinced to simply pick a number and say that their product is "valued at" that amount.[87] That amount is the biggest bunch of BS you've ever heard. People just pull a number out of the air and pretend that's the value.

Actually, they don't pull it out of the air.[88]

Conventional "wisdom"[89] says that the total value of whatever you're going to offer should be ten times the price you charge. This is the dumbest concept ever! If it's really valued at ten times the price, why are you only charging me one-tenth for this transformative training? That doesn't make a lot of sense.

Instead of simply making up a number, why not find something real? Show another way to solve their problem that, in fact, costs a lot more, whether that's ten times or twenty times more. Just make it something real that your people can believe.

If you're doing a one-to-many offer, like a course or a membership, oftentimes your alternative cost email will focus on what it would cost your audience to hire someone else to do it for them, whether that's you or someone else. That is a way to anchor it to a real price, not a BS made-up value.

Testimonials

Another email you can add is an email loaded with testimonials. If you have multiple great case studies, you may choose to send a

---

87. You can't see me right now, but I'm doing air quotes and rolling my eyes.

88. Or their ass, if that's where your mind went next.

89. More air quotes.

second case study email (either instead of this one or in addition to it). But I like to do the testimonials email slightly differently.

If you have testimonials, for example, screenshots of Facebook comments or emails, then load those screenshots into your email. If you don't have screenshots, you can just type them in.

The point of this email is to talk about all these other people who have gotten great results and who love your product. It creates more social proof because if they only read a single case study, they might think, "Oh, it worked for that person, but that's probably the exception. It's not going to work for me."

I like this to be the email that goes out after the case study email, typically the next day. Hit them with tons and tons of people who have said great things about the results they got from your product. Ideally, if you can, include testimonials from people at different stages of their journey—some who are just starting out, others who are in the middle, and other people who are more advanced. Seeing the testimonials from all these different people will help your audience see themselves in at least one of them.

It's also a great idea to include some fun language here. I had one person who said something along the lines of "the legal stuff is about as much fun as scooping your eyeballs out with a spoon or talking politics with your neighbor, but Bobby actually made it quick, easy, and kind of enjoyable." If anyone who gives you a testimonial has a way with words, include it—that will make it more memorable.

Again, don't lie. Don't make them up. These should be real people who've gotten good results from your product. But if this is the first time you're launching this product, maybe include a testimonial from someone talking about how you're an amazing teacher. In that case, you want to be clear and transparent that they're talking about *you*, not this product.

If you don't have testimonials, don't send this email. (And if you don't have testimonials yet, I want you to focus on helping people get results and then collect testimonials so you'll have them next time!) But if you do, you should.

Bobby's Swift Kick in the Ass

If you're doing an event, you'll also have to write a mini promo sequence about the event, selling people on signing up for it and then actually attending, whether virtually or in person. To get all the details on how I suggest writing this sequence, make sure you sign up at www.bobbyklinck.com/email.

A lot of people who do event-based launches spend a lot of time focusing on that event. Then at the very last minute, they think about their sales sequence emails. That's a good way to be completely overwhelmed. Your emails will be just as important as your event, especially if you've been doing everything else I've taught you so far in this book.

When I did webinar-based promotions, about 50 percent of the people who ultimately bought never signed up for or attended the webinar. They bought because they got my emails. If you do it right, your emails can be a powerful tool all on their own, so it's worth putting in the time. If you don't, you're going to miss out on a lot of those sales.

LEAVE ME ALONE!

A lot of people worry that they're going to send too many emails. If you have that worry, then I'm quite certain you won't be sending too many emails. Kinda like the people who have imposter syndrome aren't the ones who should be worried about whether they're qualified. And if you're worried you're being too sales-y, you're not.

All that being said, as a permission-based marketer, you should give people the ability to opt out of your sales sequences. In every email you send during a promo, except the very last one, you should have a link they can click to opt out of this group of promo emails.

In the past, I've done this as a PS or PPS line (you've seen some examples above). With that approach, you'll generally say something like "Over the next few days, I'm going to be sending you more emails about (description of the promotion). If you love my regular emails but would rather not hear more about this promotion, just click this link and we won't send you any more." That link then just takes them to a page telling them they are opted out. You then use the magic of the internets to apply a tag that excludes them from future emails in this one sales sequence.

In one recent promotion, I got a bit bolder with my invitation for people to opt out on cart close day. I was going to send five emails that day, so I wanted to give people an easy out. Here's the beginning part of that email:

From: Bobby Klinck

Subject: Today's the day you should unsubscribe…

Whoa… Did I really just tell you to unsubscribe?

Well, not entirely.

I just wanted you to know that today is cart close day for James Wedmore's Business By Design…

… which means I have about 157 emails coming your way today.

And if you're like most people who get my emails, you know that means you're probably going to get some wild entertainment all the livelong day.

BUT if you're over hearing about Business By Design and you're super sure you're not going to sign up, then cool.

You can <u>click here to opt out</u> of hearing from me about BBD for the rest of the year.

No hard feelings. Promise. 😊

Don't worry. You'll still get my regular weird emails.

We probably had two hundred people click that link. You might be thinking, "Oh no, that's a lot of people who didn't hear about your promotion!" But those are two hundred people *I didn't annoy the living crap out of.* I looked at the list, and they were some of my longest-term subscribers. They weren't going to buy anyway, or they already had that product—they just didn't want to hear it anymore.

Remember, we talked about treating people like friends. If a friend says stop, you honor their request.

THE JOURNEY IS AN ARC

Because different buyers will be buying at different times, they're not all going to see all of your emails. But that doesn't mean that you shouldn't plan every email from beginning to end, so they fit into an overarching theme. You should—and you get bonus points for doing so.[90]

You might be writing and sending fifteen or more emails. When you can create a thread through that entire series, instead of just seeing an unconnected email here and another random email there, people begin to see that connection. And they like it.[91]

A great way to do this is by seeding your emails with hints and clues that will pay off once your readers learn what you're going to be selling.

I did this when I was creating a product called BADA$$ Email Marketing. First, I had my audience take an assessment that helped them determine what kind of nurture sequence, welcome sequence, and sales sequence to use. Then I invited them to a webinar, where I sold them the product. (Which, by the way, you can now get for free! Head to www.bobbyklinck.com/email to sign up.)

---

90. Bonus points are redeemable for absolutely nothing except my deepest admiration.

91. One person actually said that reading through my sales emails was like reading a murder mystery!

In every email, starting in the ones about the assessment, I used language that planted seeds about being a badass email marketer—but I hadn't yet directly introduced that concept. When I invited people to the webinar, I planted seeds that made them think, "Hey, I want to be a badass!" Then, as they read further, they thought, "I want to be a badass at email!"

Finally, when they heard that there's a program called BADA$$ Email Marketing, those seeds that had been planted in their mind all along suddenly bore fruit. The people who read these emails didn't recognize the theme up front. It was just subconscious messaging in their brains. But as time went along, it started to make more sense.

Think through the entire process, from the very beginning to the final result you want, and you can take your audience on a powerful journey—a journey that ends with more sales!

WHEN IN DOUBT, SEND ANOTHER EMAIL

When in doubt, send another email—you'll feel like you're sending a lot, but don't stop.

Guess what?

Getting someone to buy is not the end of the journey. You should continue to think through how to treat them right with email.

If you've followed my guidance so far and you're sending weekly emails that are serving your people, I'm not worried. You're going to take care of them and send them the information they need. Even if they don't buy right now, they're going to get your weekly emails again, so they'll still be in the process of being nurtured and served by you.

Continue to treat them well and they will become your brand advocates—and raving fans.

CONCLUSION

ALTHOUGH I'M A TRUE BELIEVER THAT THE ONLY superhero worth listening to is Deadpool,[92] one of my teammates always reminds me of this quote from *Spider-Man*: "With great power comes great responsibility."

Reading this book, you now have great power. You need to use it responsibly. And whatever you do, don't use it against me like one of my *first* email marketing students did:

From: Lynnelle Sell

To: Bobby Klinck

Subject: Listening to your podcast, I almost drove off the road...

Bobby,

I love the TV show *Suits*. Just discovered it during the Pandemic.

My life is so interesting that Suits has turned into an evening ritual...

...and I'm actually excited about it!

(continued on page 226)

---

92. Given all the snark and breaking the fourth wall in this book, is this really any surprise?!?!

(continued from page 225)

Harvey Specter is a bada$$ attorney (see what I did there) who always finds a smart or creative way to win his cases.

You're probably wondering why I'm telling you about Suits...

Well, as I was listening to your Tuesday podcast, I almost drove off the road.

I learned that you were giving people free tickets to BOM Live if they purchased the Template Library in August....

....which is a fantastic offer and extremely generous BUT there's one problem.

I purchased the Template Library on July, 16th. UGH!

Two weeks! How do I get the last 2 weeks of July moved to August?

I need to channel my inner Harvey Specter and find some loophole, precedent, or angle to get a free ticket to BOM Live.

Only problem...I'm negotiating with a Harvard educated lawyer.

Maybe, somehow, there is a way to be grandfathered in? Is there an appeal process? How 'bout a class action?

O.K., I'm all out of the legal terminology I've picked up from Suits.

Just thought I'd throw that out there... and practice my BEM email skills.

Bobby, just hit reply and let me know your thoughts.

See you at 1pm!

Lynnelle Sell

(continued on page 227)

(continued from page 226)

P.S. Regardless of your decision, I'm super excited about what I've learned in BEM. BTW...this is the fastest Story-Based Email I've written so far.

P.P.S. Suits is on Amazon Prime. I highly recommend it.

I freaking trained Lynnelle to write an email there was *no way* I could say no to. So, like I said...don't use your newfound powers against me. 'Cause that would be supremely uncool.

Kidding aside, there's an important reason I got Lynnelle's permission to include that email in this conclusion.

If you're like a lot of the entrepreneurs I've worked with on email writing, you read the emails in this book and thought to yourself, "Well, Bobby's clearly a natural storyteller, but I could never write emails like that." Did I get that about right?

Lynnelle is proof that it's not just me. She wrote that email after she had been working through my email marketing program (the one that's now free) for about three months. And that is a damn good email, if I do say so myself.

But it's not just Lynnelle. I could tell you about Mackenzie, who is a health coach who always gets me to read her emails about donuts, bacon, pizza, and who the hell knows what else. Or my friend Jamie, who is an entrepreneur who serves school-teachers and sent an email with the subject line "I love it more than Dicks." Yep. True story.

These entrepreneurs and countless others have embraced email marketing that doesn't suck. They're having fun writing their emails, and their audiences are eating it up.

That's what's possible when you embrace what you've learned in this book.

ONE OF US, ONE OF US

If you're still reading this and you're not on my list yet, what's wrong with you? You can have even more of my writing! If you haven't yet joined my community, now's the time.

Go to www.bobbyklinck.com/email to find lots more examples of emails, full swipe files, and an easy way to sign up for my free BAD@$$ Email Marketing course. That course is updated periodically to include my most current thinking about specific tactics and strategies that you can use from start to finish on your email marketing journey.

Follow me on Instagram (@BobbyKlinck) and join my free Facebook group: www.Facebook.com/groups/badassonlinemarketers.

But whether you choose to sign up for my emails, join the free course, or follow me on social media, please don't ignore my *most important* piece of advice:

Just *start*.

Don't wait until you have a great nurture sequence and the perfect welcome sequence. I'd rather you write your CATCH email and then start sending weekly emails to people instead of holding off until everything is ready. Don't get lost in the weeds, trying to do everything but actually accomplishing nothing.

Understand that your journey through email marketing is a work in progress—and it always will be. The most important moment of a journey is the first step, so go out there and get started!

YOU ARE READY

If you're still reading this, you clearly like reading what I have to write,[93] so by now you may be realizing that I just might know what I'm talking about. This book is written very much how I write emails—and how you should be writing emails too.

Now you know what to do. You've become friends with your audience. Your people know, like, and trust you. You enjoy writing to them, because they enjoy reading what you write. They're interested in you as a person, but they're also interested in ways that you can help them.

Have I convinced you yet that email marketing doesn't have to suck?

I'm hoping that email isn't scary anymore. You're no longer facing a blinking cursor that is mocking you. Instead, a blank email is the opportunity to have some *fun*.

You now have a roadmap, so you're not lost on your journey through email marketing. You have your GPS, and it's telling you exactly where to go.

Remember how crappy my emails used to be? (If not, just go back and reread the Introduction.) I used to be mind-numbingly boring…but I'm not anymore, and you don't have to be either!

---

93. If not, seriously, why are you still here? Why did you read every word of this book if you didn't like it?

ACKNOWLEDGMENTS

THIS BOOK WOULD NOT HAVE BEEN POSSIBLE WITHOUT the contributions of so many people. All the people I mentioned in the book played a role in my journey, and I owe them a debt of gratitude. There's no way I could possibly thank everyone who played a role personally, but there are some people who deserve special thanks.

This book started with a conversation in the wee hours of the night after my team and I wrapped up our first-ever virtual event—BADA$$ Online Marketing Live. It all started with this discussion between me and Katie Chase (my number two, who makes everything in my business possible):

Katie: "I'm just sitting here in awe of all the things that had to come together to make the last three days possible. I mean, think about it. A worldwide pandemic and still our business has doubled. Because of COVID, people were hungrier for connection than ever before. They were so ready for what we wanted to give. A beautiful movement to start during a global crisis. It's all working together for us."

Me: "Yep. Can I write my book now?"

Katie: "Go for it. Eat that cake!"[94]

Katie probably envisioned an inspiring book about being a radical giver who chooses the serve-first approach to entrepreneurship. Instead, we ended up with a snark-filled book about email marketing. Maybe inspiration comes in the second book?

Katie, you are an amazing human being who makes everything possible for me and this crazy business we are building. Calling you my number two does not do you justice. I'm so thankful that you came into my world in 2018 and that you were silly enough to say yes to managing my rebrand in 2019. Convincing you to join my team is, hands down, the smartest thing I've ever done in business. You're the Gus to my Shawn. I can say without hesitation that my business would not be what it is today without you by my side. But you're so much more than a team member. My life would not be as rich as it is if I didn't know you. At this point, you're my coach, my confidant, and my friend. Thank you for everything you've done for me, Katie!

Next up, thanks to all the students who've trusted me to teach them a thing or two about email marketing through the years. The people who took a risk on me when I first launched the FANS First Society and those who chose to join BADA$$ Email Marketing from me *right as* COVID was getting real. (I literally sent the first email inviting people to my sales webinar the day that would eventually be remembered as the day the NBA suspended games, Tom Hanks announced his diagnosis, and the President announced he was shutting down travel from Europe.)

---

94. We have an inside joke where Katie constantly insists that I "eat my vegetables" before eating the cake. It's her way of telling me to do what *has* to be done before doing the fun stuff.

If you are one of the original BEM students, you are responsible for this book. Here's hoping you think that's a good thing.

Thank you to my amazing editor and writing partner, Jenny Shipley. I loved breaking the book-writing process with you. Hopefully, readers figured out you aren't really a party pooper. This book would not exist without you, so thank you, Jenny!

Thank you to Tarzan Kay, my original email teacher and mentor. Your teaching put me on the path to becoming the email marketer I am today…and your message saying I have the "X factor on steroids" is the only reason I'm doing anything beyond helping people with the legal stuff. I am forever in your debt, my friend!

What can I say about my favorite Aussie, Jillian Bowen? Thank you for making sure my head never gets too big, and thank you for telling me to send that now-famous photobomb email. I'm anxiously awaiting the day when travel is easier so we can hang out at another entrepreneur event. Thank you for everything, Jillian.

Thank you to my friend Melanie Howe. Just think; that silly "more cowbell" comment you made to me more than three years ago is the only reason the world knows the real Bobby. Although some people might be cursing you for that, I'm eternally grateful. 'Cause being boring sucks! Thank you for everything, Melanie.

Thanks to my brother, Chris. You taught me one of the most important lessons I've ever learned: that it's worth getting in trouble to stand up for people you care about. The ripple effect of that lesson is being felt by all the people who I'm helping today. Thank you for being the best big brother a guy could ask for.

Thanks to Bobbi Jo Curty and Shelley Madueme for being part of Team Klinck. You help Katie keep me under control.

More importantly, you help me change the lives of thousands of entrepreneurs. Thank you for everything you do.

Thanks to Ellie Cole and the other amazing people at Scribe Media. Your hard work is what made this book happen.

Last, but certainly not least, thank you to my wife, Kristy. More than anyone, you've experienced the wild ride that is my life. You've been with me through high school, college, law school, the lost decades when I was a boring lawyer, and the last four years of me building this online business. You've survived five cross-country moves and were the first one to believe that I could build my own business. Thank you for supporting my crazy idea to stop with the whole "being a lawyer" thing to build a business and life I actually enjoy. I love everything about you and am blessed to have you by my side.

ABOUT THE AUTHOR

BOBBY KLINCK is a Harvard Law grad turned online entrepreneur—but he's *not* your typical lawyer. He doesn't do suits, he hates legalese more than you do, and he has a tendency to make ridiculous pop-culture references and dad jokes.

He's built a thriving online business by doing things a bit differently than other people…making the legal and business stuff simple, with a focus on building real connections with real people instead of thinking of people as potential transactions.

After trying the "secret" strategies all the "expert" online entrepreneurs were telling him to do, Bobby threw out the "online marketing" rulebook and started marketing his way…by giving, connecting with his audience, and building his brand. Throwing out the rulebook helped Bobby skyrocket his business success.

Along the way, he discovered that email marketing is one of the most powerful ways to connect with his audience and build his brand. After hearing countless people ask him how he made email marketing work, he decided to start teaching it to other online business owners.

Nowadays, he helps online entrepreneurs with email marketing, marketing more generally, and the legal stuff. And he's adopted a crazy idea he calls "radical giving," which involves giving away nearly all his trainings for free. You can learn more at www.bobbyklinck.com.

Printed in Great Britain
by Amazon

18984427R00154